GERMANY AND AMERICA

GERMANY AND AMERICA

New Identities, Fateful Rift?

W. R. Smyser

with a Foreword by Paul Nitze

Westview Press

BOULDER · SAN FRANCISCO · OXFORD

Copyright © 1993 by Westview Press, Inc.

Published in 1993 in the United States of America by Westview Press, Inc., 5500 Central Avenue, Boulder, Colorado 80301-2877, and in the United Kingdom by Westview Press, 36 Lonsdale Road, Summertown, Oxford OX2 7EW

An earlier version was published in 1992 in German as *Deutschland gegen Amerika?* by Rombach Verlag.

Library of Congress Cataloging-in-Publication Data
Smyser, W. R., 1931–
    Germany and America : new identities, fateful rift? / W. R. Smyser; with a foreword by Paul Nitze.
        p.   cm.
    Includes index.
    ISBN 0-8133-1861-0. — ISBN 0-8133-1862-9 (pbk.)
        1. United States—Foreign relations—Germany.   2. Germany—Foreign relations—United States.   3. Germany—Foreign relations—1990–
4. United States—Foreign relations—1989–1993.   5. United States—Foreign relations—1993–   I. Title.
E183.8.G3S585   1993
327.73043—dc20   93-11276
                                                                                                CIP

Printed and bound in the United States of America

The paper used in this publication meets the requirements
of the American National Standard for Permanence of Paper
for Printed Library Materials Z39.48-1984.

10   9   8   7   6   5   4   3   2   1

CONTENTS

PART THREE
THE GERMANY THAT CAN SAY NO

FOREWORD

Paul Nitze

This is an important book, one that looks at the past in a new way and one that also warns about the future. I think it is right to do both.

Smyser does not follow the customary approach to the German-American relationship. He does not see it only as a bilateral link between two important countries, or even as only a part of the North Atlantic system.

Instead, Smyser sees the German-American relationship as an important and integral element in a worldwide alliance structure that has stretched from Japan to Berlin for forty years. That alliance system has been composed of maritime powers such as the United States and continental powers such as Germany, and it has therefore reflected the interests of both.

The maritime powers have always had their own wide view of the world. They did not want to be trapped on any continent such as Europe, but they also did not want a hostile power to take control of any continent. Continental powers have always wanted to use the maritime powers to help them against their other continental rivals.

The global system, which Smyser calls the global concert, is now at risk of breaking apart. Neither the maritime nor the continental powers need each other as much as they did.

Smyser reviews what has happened since German unification and analyzes what it might mean for the ties between Germany and the maritime powers and for the ties between America and the continental states. He warns that Germany and America are on a path that can lead to a major split in the alliance system.

Smyser's argument should bring us back to two important moments in postwar history:

The first was the period between 1945 and 1955, when Washington was creating the North Atlantic alliance as well as the treaty with Japan. During those years, a global alliance system was at the center of our strategic thought. Germany and Europe were important, but we wanted to do more than build a transatlantic pact. We wanted to create a world at peace and were prepared to do what was necessary to help build and defend it.

The second moment was the negotiation of the détente and arms control agreements with Moscow during the 1970s and 1980s before the breakup of the Soviet Union. In those years we also saw those treaties in global terms. We did not negotiate only for the safety and stability of Europe, although we were often negotiating about weapons systems that were deployed in Europe. We were interested in making the whole world safe.

Even during those periods, there was always a risk that the global alliance would not hold. After the war, we were not certain that we could keep together a firm alliance between the American and the European continents. Many Americans did not want us involved in Europe. Many Europeans thought we would not stay long enough to keep them safe.

During détente, Europeans as well as Americans feared that arms control and any relaxation of tensions would sap our will to defend ourselves. But such fissures as did appear in the alliance were repaired.

We are now at an even more serious moment, as Smyser points out. Bonn and Washington could make mistakes of truly historic proportions. Germany is for the first time in the twentieth century a victorious power, and it needs to decide how to use that power to help build a safe and stable world. The United States has to remember its own successful principles of action and commitment. Although we may all need each other less than we did thirty years ago, the world has not changed enough to permit a retreat into isolationism or petty quarreling with friends.

Smyser looks at the record and shows that the maritime and continental powers have begun to pull apart, and that Germany and the United States have not recently worked together as effectively as during the cold war. He warns of recent trends in German and American economic and military policies, and he points out that these developments not only run the risk of splitting Bonn and Washington but of splitting the global alliance system.

This book therefore goes well beyond German-American relations. It makes us look at the future organization of the world and at the future defense not only of the West but also of the entire global political structure that the United States and Germany as well as others have built.

The book also warns that we risk frittering away once again an immense triumph that we won with great effort. We may repeat the error that we and others have made in the past, breaking up the alliances that helped us win great victories and then wondering why our achievements proved so transitory.

As Smyser points out, the Americans and the Germans will probably have more to do with the future direction of the world than any other two nations. We can only hope that they will act wisely.

PREFACE

The subtitle of this book poses a question. It is a difficult question to have to ask after four decades of close German-American cooperation.

There is no conclusive answer now. But the question must still be posed.

The Federal Republic of Germany and the United States have been close and even intimate allies since the formation of the West German state, although they have had their share of arguments. They have worked together to shape the basic elements of the global political, economic, and military system.

The foundations on which the close German-American relationship was built have now collapsed. New ones are being built, albeit slowly. Relations therefore must change, and they will. The only question is how.

If the two governments want to maintain a close relationship, they must do two things: first, examine and define new foundations for a relationship; second, and perhaps as important, follow policies that will reinforce their relationship rather than weaken it.

To set the stage, I will begin the book by looking at the new world and the new Europe, the basic arenas in which German-American relations play themselves out. In the first part of the book, I will also describe the new America and the new Germany as well as their new mutual identities.

In the second part of the book, I will review German-American relations since German unification in 1990. That should enable the reader to determine how the transition from the old to the new relationship is being managed.

In the third and final part, I shall draw the appropriate conclusions.

German-American relations are always in motion. Even as this book goes to press, many subjects in this book are being discussed among Germans, Americans, and others. Consultations and negotiations go on all the time.

A new American president, Bill Clinton, has come into office. He is interested in Germany and regards Germany as a potential model for America in some ways.

Even President Clinton cannot, however, change the fundamental situation. And it is that situation, the shift in the very foundations of German-American relations, that is now driving the relationship. Only a common and concerted effort can direct that shift.

A first version of this book was published in Germany by Rombach Verlag at the end of 1992 under the title "Deutschland gegen Amerika?" This American edition is updated and includes several new elements that have emerged between the publication of the German book and the completion of this manuscript.

W. R. Smyser

Part One

NEW PARTNERS
IN A NEW ARENA

1

MEETINGS IN CAMP DAVID, WASHINGTON, AND MUNICH

On the weekend of March 21 and 22, 1992, Chancellor Helmut Kohl of the Federal Republic of Germany visited President George Bush of the United States at the president's weekend retreat at Camp David. They met in this informal setting to review German-American relations and to discuss some urgent problems. They spoke quietly and directly, with few assistants, for several hours each day, being old friends as well as world leaders.

After the meeting, the two held a press briefing at which they said that they had talked in a positive spirit and that relations between Germany and the United States were strong and friendly. Kohl even went so far as to endorse Bush for reelection, telling the press that Bush's successful conduct of American foreign policy should be an important factor in his favor.

After the summit ended, however, it became clear that the meeting represented a very peculiar paradox. On the one hand, the leaders did meet and speak in a highly positive and friendly atmosphere. They agreed that German-American relations were excellent. On the other hand, the details of their press briefings showed that they reached no agreement on a number of crucial questions.

Kohl asked Bush to join in inviting Russian president Boris Yeltsin to attend the Munich summit of the global industrial powers (the G-7) in July 1992. Bush made no commitment at that time. Kohl also asked Bush to pledge significant U.S. aid to Russia and to other states of the new Commonwealth of Independent States (CIS) that had replaced the Soviet Union. Again, Bush made no commitment. Several weeks later, he announced a major American share in an international aid program to Russia, but the timing of his announcement showed that he was acting more in response to pressure at home than to support Yeltsin or to agree with Kohl.

The most important single problem that the two leaders discussed at Camp David was the future of world trade, and especially the problem of agricultural subsidies paid to European farmers by the European Community. On this, there was also no meeting of the minds. Both the American and the German delegations said that the president and the chancellor failed to agree on the kind of changes in European agricultural policies that would permit liberalized trade in world food products.

3

When the press asked Chancellor Kohl about agriculture after the meeting, he replied that he had not brought the authority to negotiate this question because he only represented one member of the European Community and could not speak for all. He added pointedly that concessions had to be made on all sides, a remark that was widely interpreted as a recommendation to President Bush.

Bush must have been bitterly disappointed. The White House had been saying privately for a year and a half that Kohl had committed himself at the G-7 summit in Houston, Texas, in the summer of 1990, to solve this problem by persuading other European governments to accept changes in their agricultural policies. At the time of the Houston summit, the United States had been energetically supporting German unification and Kohl had been hoping to win re-election that fall as the "chancellor of unity."

A month after the Camp David meeting, in April 1992, Bush met with the president of the European Commission, Jacques Delors, and with the Portuguese president of the Community's Council of Ministers. They also discussed the agricultural trade problem. They did not reach agreement either. Delors let it be known to the press that he was only an international civil servant and that he did not have the authority to negotiate changes in Community agriculture policies. His delegation pointed out that he certainly did not have as much authority to change those policies as did the chancellor of the Community's most powerful member, Germany, who had only recently himself met with President Bush.

If Bush was hoping to win votes from American farmers for his own 1992 re-election campaign by a successful negotiation on farm questions, Kohl and the new united Germany had not helped him at Camp David.

The meetings underlined that the world of 1992 was not the world of the cold war. For the questions that Bush and Kohl had to resolve were primarily economic, such as trade and aid, not the kind of geopolitical and strategic issues on which American presidents and German chancellors had concentrated their conversations during the cold war.

The meeting between the chancellor and the president also provided an additional insight into the new world. Kohl and Bush had met as two equal partners, and Kohl did not need to make any concessions on issues that he and other Europeans regarded as important. He did not even need to make the kinds of concessions and promises that he had made in 1990 when he needed support for German unification and when Germany still needed U.S. protection.

But Kohl was not the only German to come to America. At the end of April, President Richard von Weizsäcker came to pay a state visit. He had originally scheduled that visit in 1991 as the very first state visit that he would make after German independence because he wanted to thank the American people for their support of German unity over the years. The visit had to be postponed to 1992 because the disagreement between Germany and the United States about the German role in the Gulf crisis made it inappropriate during 1991.

President von Weizsäcker's visit happened to coincide with the American celebration of Holocaust Day, an annual memorial to the Jewish victims of the Nazi Holocaust. He was invited to attend a Holocaust memorial service in the U.S. capitol, a signal honor for a German. During the day and evening of his state visit, the Washington press and television was dominated by recollections of the Holocaust, with a three-hour television special on the Polish concentration camp at Lodz.

Like the chancellor's visit, President von Weizsäcker's proceeded in a positive spirit, although the protocol and political attention was not at the level at which it might have been for the leader of one of the most important states in the world. Like President Bush, von Weizsäcker spoke of the importance and the promise of the German-American relationship. He thanked America for its support of Germany and pledged continued cooperation. Yet the emphasis, especially in the unplanned connection with the Holocaust, was on the past instead of on the future.

On the same day, however, Chancellor Kohl met in Bonn with Japanese premier Kiichi Miyazawa. They agreed that their two countries should play more influential roles in world politics because of their economic power. As the German president was recollecting the past in Washington, the German chancellor was projecting the future in Bonn. The reality of German contrition was evolving into the reality of German power.

Two more German ministers were to come to Washington during 1992: the new minister of foreign affairs, Klaus Kinkel, and the new minister of defense, Volker Rühe. During their meetings with American officials, they explained why Germany would help constitute a new Franco-German Corps, which the U.S. government saw as a potential threat to NATO. They both explained that these fears were unfounded and that they would go ahead with the Corps. The German Information Service reported that the talks had been harmonious despite the disagreements.

In July, Kohl and Bush met again at the Munich G-7 summit. By then, President Bush had changed his mind about Russia. He not only promised aid to Russia but he even suggested informally that Russia should join the G-7 to make it the G-8. The chancellor opposed the suggestion as premature. Bush also wanted to conclude or at least advance several basic issues in the Uruguay Round trade negotiations at Munich, but Kohl opposed any such discussion because he saw it as fruitless and thought it would disrupt the meeting's positive spirit and perhaps jeopardize a French referendum on European unity scheduled for September. Once again, the German and American leaders disagreed—although they tried hard not to make it obvious to others.

All these meetings and events mark a new world, a world in which united Germany and the United States must look again at their relationship. The United States is changing. Germany is changing. Much around them is changing as well. The past, the present, and the future all fuse into a kaleidoscope which shows sharp and apparently clear images in different colors but which does not permit the observer to see behind the colors at what lies ahead.

The kaleidoscope does, however, invite some sobering questions as the past and the future mingle. For the new politics of Europe, Asia, and America are not the old. The old problems, the old obligations, and the old opportunities are not the new.

The new German-American relations are plainly not the old either. There has been the usual ritual of harmonious discussions and the usual litany of mutual assurances, but the meetings have been marked more by disagreement than by agreement.

One cannot help but wonder what such meetings mean. One cannot help but ask how Germany and America will now cooperate when they seem not to agree on major questions. And one cannot avoid reflecting on what might happen if the atmosphere in German-American meetings begins to reflect the present and the future more than the past, or if the many pressures now surrounding the relationship could distort and reshape its focus.

Finally, and perhaps most significant, was the meeting that did not take place. When Bush returned from Moscow in January 1993, completing his last trip as president, he did not stop in Bonn. Instead, he flew to Paris to see French president François Mitterrand.

It was, perhaps, an ominous final sign of the state of German-American relations. The president who had begun his term by talking about German-American "partnership in leadership" ended it by flying over Germany to stop in Paris.

Ironically, during that same month, the U.S. government held a special ceremony in Berlin to mark its rebuilding plans for the former American Embassy on the Pariser Platz, only yards away from where the Wall had stood. America thus marked the importance of Germany and Berlin at the center of Europe even as the American president and the German chancellor no longer had anything to say to each other.

On March 26, 1993, Kohl met with the new American president, Bill Clinton, for a get-acquainted visit in Washington. Both men had been somewhat nervous about the meeting: Kohl because he had been known to favor Bush over Clinton during the 1992 election, and Clinton because he was new to foreign policy and wanted his first meeting to go well.

As it was, the first meeting went well indeed. The two men greeted each other warmly and were wreathed in smiles during the press conference that followed their meeting. It became clear during that press conference, however, that they had not settled any of the issues that had troubled German-American relations during Bush's final years in office. They expressed good intentions, and they met in a positive atmosphere, but they did not remove German-American differences. That work remained before them, even if the good intentions might be regarded as a positive sign.

These are sequences that Germans and Americans might well ponder as they examine their common victory and the new world that they have created together and in which they must now try to work together. What are the things that now matter for Germany and America? Can Germans and Americans work together to solve them? Why did a personal relationship of so much promise end as it did? What might it mean for the future of both countries? Finally, of course, where do they go from here?

2

THE VICTORY OF
THE GLOBAL CONCERT

The world changed dramatically around the turn of the 1990s through four sepa-rate but connected events: the collapse of the Communist system in Eastern Europe during the latter 1980s; the breach of the Berlin Wall in November, 1989; the unification of Germany in October, 1990; and the failure of the military coup in the Soviet Union in August, 1991, with the subsequent disintegration of the Soviet imperium.

The collapse of the Soviet Union and of its European bulwark marked a vic-tory for the great international coalition that had been assembled after World War II, between 1945 and 1955.

At the core of that international coalition stood an association of states, which for want of a better term can be called the global concert. That global concert is the association of the principal industrialized democracies of the world.

The global concert is not a shapeless, amorphous mass. It is a small number of states that attempt to direct or at least to shape what happens across most of the world. The concert has existed for several centuries. It has evolved as the world has evolved, and it has not always had the same members. It is informal, little recognized, and little understood, but it has wielded immense influence and power.

The global concert was established and has been maintained by the maritime democracies, with Great Britain originally at its center. Because it is an informal structure, one cannot fix a specific date for its creation, but it emerged slowly during the seventeenth and eighteenth centuries after the great age of discovery gave a lasting advantage to those states that could command the seas and thus the resources of the world as a whole.

Great Britain led the concert during most of its existence, but the United States gradually assumed the leading role during the twentieth century. America became an equal partner with England during the 1920s and 1930s. It became the recognized leader of the concert during the late 1940s, as Great Britain faltered after having exhausted itself in World War II.

Contrary to the hopes and expectations of most Americans, the United States did not come to enjoy a long and stable peace after 1945. Instead, Washington found itself having to direct, manage, and finance the most widespread and far-reaching combination of military, political, and economic operations of all time for the broad purpose of what came to be known as "containment." Those operations, culminating in the cold war victory, involved not only the global concert itself but many others who supported or joined it.

During the cold war, because of the challenge to the Atlantic powers from the Soviet Union to the east, the global concert and its allies were often known as the Western alliance despite the presence of Japan. But the concert has always had global interests, a global presence, and a sense of global mission. It has been a world coalition. The close identification of most of its members with the oceans gave them a perspective different from that of the land powers, who had to concentrate on the management of their immediate surroundings and the protection of their borders.

The events of 1989–1991 represented the third victory that the global concert won against continental powers in Europe during the twentieth century. It may prove to be decisive, especially if the members of the concert can hold together as successfully in peace as they did in war.

The states that created the global concert, and those that have directed it, have not been selfless. They have generally reserved places in the concert only for those in their own image, which has been democratic and capitalist. They have also tried, sometimes successfully and sometimes unsuccessfully, to shape the world as a whole to serve their own interests, needs and wishes. They have been willing to adjust the global system somewhat to suit others, and the system has been able to accommodate and incorporate many nations. The concert's capacity to find heterogeneous allies has accounted in large measure for its endurance and for its successes.

The states of the global concert have not, however, been prepared to accept defiance. They have not yielded to what they have perceived as challenges to the concert itself or to the system that it created. They have not wanted to let the world deviate from their political and economic principles or to let a new system replace their own.

The states of the global concert have fought and beaten back threats from several European continental challengers, such as Napoleon, Wilhelm II, Hitler, or the Soviet Union—usually at immense cost to themselves as well as to their opponents. They have also fought off challenges in Asia, whether from Japan or China. One reason for their successes in Europe has been their ability to find allies on the continent itself. No single European state has ever been able to control and mobilize the resources of the entire continent against the global powers, although France, Germany, and Russia tried to do so and even came close at times.

During much of the nineteenth and twentieth centuries, Germany's leaders as well as many other Germans believed—whether rightly or wrongly—that the global system was oriented against them. They thought that Germany had not been conceded, and would not be conceded, its proper place. Germany could not join the global concert on its own terms. It was, despite its power and influence, not invited to help direct the global system. Its political structure, its unpredictability, and the apparently overweening ambitions of its leaders frightened the maritime states, who were more ready to cooperate with other democracies than with strong-willed monarchs and dictators.

Kaiser Wilhelm II and Chancellor Adolf Hitler openly rejected the principles of the global concert and tried to impose their own. Whatever their respective claims and objectives may have been, the outcomes were clear. Both times, Germany was defeated.

After the second German defeat, and during Germany's occupation, the Western parts of Germany became part of the global concert and of the democratic global system. The Federal Republic of Germany joined the maritime democracies, America and England, and their allies. As it did so, it enabled the global concert to reach into the center of Europe, and even to Berlin itself, for the first time in history. It did so because there was no other way to protect the Western remnants of Germany from Stalin's empire. Never before had an alliance system stretched so far and wide, from the far shores and waters of the Pacific Ocean to the Elbe and the Spree rivers.

In order to organize and to coordinate their efforts, the maritime democracies and their friends created a panoply of international organizations. Some of them were established even before the end of World War II. Others were to follow as the crisis in Europe and elsewhere became clear in the immediate years after the world war. Some of the organizations were economic. Others were military or political. But they all served to hold the vast alliance system together and to give them a common stake in unity.

Not all of the organizations established by the global concert have survived, but many have, with the following playing the most important roles:

- For global economic coordination, the World War II allies established the World Bank and the International Monetary Fund (IMF) during a meeting at the New Hampshire resort of Bretton Woods in 1944. At that meeting, they also established a global monetary system based upon fixed exchange rates and a firm link between the U.S. dollar and gold, although that link was to break down by 1971.
- For trade, they established the General Agreement on Tariffs and Trade (GATT) in 1947, a system that has been periodically widened and deepened since then by a series of negotiating rounds.
- For more detailed economic consultations among the industrialized states, they established the Organization for Economic Cooperation and Development (OECD), which had originally been created to coordinate the European side of the Marshall Plan.
- For the defense of the Atlantic area and Western Europe, the Atlantic states created the North Atlantic Treaty Organization (NATO).

- For their common interests in Asia, Japan and the United States signed a treaty of their own, adjusting it as necessary over time.

Each of those organizations had its function. But the concert initially lacked a single central organization that could be used for world-wide policy coordination and consultation. The United Nations, originally conceived for that purpose, had been split by the cold war. Nothing had been put in its place.

Such a structure finally evolved during the 1970s as the American-dominated Bretton Woods system broke down and worldwide economic coordination became essential. What then emerged, during the height of the Vietnam War and severe global economic dislocation, was an unprecedented informal council that continues to function even after the cold war victory, although it is not as strong as it was during the 1970s and 1980s.

This council does not solve problems and often does not produce agreement, but it enables the leading states of the world to consult and sometimes even to coordinate in a setting in which they are not obliged to conform to any particular set of rules or mandates. It constitutes a convenient mechanism in which the major states of the global concert can meet with an open agenda and can talk about matters basic to the relationship.

That council, which has become the true board of governors of the global system, is the Group of Seven, or the G-7. It was originally founded to coordinate international financial policy after the end of the Bretton Woods system, but it has over time been given a much wider mandate. It has also gone through several evolutionary stages as its functions and its membership have changed.

Because of its global reach and its respect for German influence and power, the global concert invited West Germany to join this board of governors from the time the board was first established. West Germany was one of the founding members of the Library Group, a group of finance ministers that first met in the White House library in 1973 after the collapse of the fixed-rate exchange mechanism two years earlier. When the Library Group became known as the Group of Five, or the G-5, West Germany was a member along with the United States, Great Britain, France and Japan. West Germany remained a member when Canada and Italy joined the G-5 to make it the G-7.

German membership in the G-7 is an immensely important matter. It is, in fact, unprecedented. For the first time in history, a united Germany has held and kept a sustained membership in a global coalition of powers. It never did so before World War I and only very briefly during the 1920s.

Although the G-7 originally had an economic mandate and purpose, it came to address issues that shaped the future of the world as a whole. It was the G-7 that coordinated global policy during the 1980s, the crucial final confrontation with the Soviet system. After the collapse of that system, it was the G-7 that gave the successor states of the Soviet Union a chance to survive by deciding in 1991 to defer Soviet debt. It is the G-7 that decides on aid and trade with the former states of the Soviet Union. It discusses global trade and financial issues and coordinates them whenever possible.

The G-7 also discusses political and strategic questions. Crises or nuclear proliferation in the Middle East, Europe, or Asia are now more likely to be first discussed within the G-7 mechanism than in any other forum. Security matters that are brought before the U.N. Security Council are often initially discussed among the G-7 states, as are many other similar questions in a continuing consultation process that goes on almost around the clock. Most recently, the G-7 has attempted to coordinate policy on the Yugoslav crisis.

The G-7 is the supreme political product of the technology age. It functions by the telephone, the fax machine, the global satellite system, and the jet aircraft, all the instruments that permit modern leaders to talk continually and to meet wherever they like on short notice. The means of diplomacy have finally caught up with the means of war.

The G-7 took over the role of coordinating the global system for several reasons:

- The G-7 includes the victors of the cold war, not the victors of World War II, and thus includes the true powers in the world. Because Japan and Germany are members, the G-7 mirrors the reality of the world better than does the U.N. Security Council.
- The economic policies that are primarily discussed in the G-7 are increasingly perceived as the most important issues facing the world. They must be solved if national legitimacy and global stability are to be protected. The G-7 agenda, therefore, reflects the real world as much as its membership does.
- The G-7's only regularly scheduled meeting is an annual summit, originally known as the economic summit. The 1992 summit was held in Munich and the 1993 summit was held in Tokyo. The summits have become elaborately and even excessively orchestrated, but most G-7 gatherings are unplanned, scheduled when and where they are needed and at the right level for the decisions to be made and the subjects to be discussed. Meetings at appropriate levels take place often, as do discreet personal consultations. The G-7 can, therefore, coordinate even on highly urgent, acute and sensitive problems.

A number of proposals have been made to formalize the G-7 mechanism, perhaps by establishing a secretariat and permanent representatives. But the members like things the way they are, informal, discreet, controlled by them and not by the bureaucracies or the media.

The G-7 has suffered the consequences of the end of the cold war as have other international coordinating mechanisms established by the global concert. The summits that have taken place since the collapse of the Berlin Wall have tended to be perfunctory and indecisive. There has been a growing sense that the mechanism needs reform, although the problem lies not mainly with the mechanism but with the reluctance of the members to coordinate as before.

For Germany, however, the G-7 has been of the highest importance. It represents the final achievement of a German seat at the most important table. For the G-7 carries more weight and more influence than does the U.N. Security Council, on which Germany does not sit. It also has the promise of evolving to meet the needs of the future as well as of today.

The global concert, with America and Germany as prominent members, has won the great battle of the cold war. It was able to do that while also reshaping much of the world outside the Communist system. It must now, however, deal with the problems of the peace, including the problems left by the disintegrating Soviet system itself.

This victory is also immensely important for Germany. For the first time in the twentieth century, Germany is the victor in a great confrontation, not the loser. For the first time, Germany can help to shape the future of the world as a victorious power. Germans are not isolated, outcast, and alone; they are at the most important table.

This truth, inadequately understood in Germany, marks the most important departure in German history from the days of the empire and of the other German governments that have succeeded it. It is to the immense credit of the United States that Americans helped to make that new German role possible.

Like other victories, however, the cold war victory is fragile. Like other victories, it also represents an obligation as well as a triumph. For the United States and Germany must now together shape the future of the world and of their relationship.

Most important, Germany and the other members of the G-7 must decide how the global alliance system itself is to be re-shaped after its great victory in order to avoid the disintegration that has so often followed success.

3

THE NEW WORLD

The new world that Germany and the United States have helped create is very different from the one in which they first began to cooperate during the late 1940s. It is not the bipolar world of the cold war. It is newer in some ways, more ancient in others. It is the world of the twenty-first century, but also the world of the nineteenth century. Paradoxically, it is both more stable than the cold war and yet potentially more dangerous.

In that new world, the democracies no longer need each other as much as they did during the cold war. The fearsome mix of Communist ideology and Soviet imperialism has been beaten back. Marxism-Leninism is finished as a motivating force in global affairs. The great empire that Lenin and Stalin assembled has crumbled. Not only do the democracies no longer need to protect themselves against the Soviet threat, but they no longer need to see all international problems in terms of that threat.

With the removal of that threat, the world can return to a less mobilized existence. Strategic and military demands and considerations no longer must prevail over all others. Economic considerations again become more important. States can turn their attention to pressing domestic problems as well as toward some new and equally pressing international matters.

Future historians may someday write that most of the twentieth century, from 1914 to 1990, represented a particularly violent and perilous phase of human history, a 75-year war for European domination. Those years saw two world wars, the cold war itself, and countless crises—often linked, as well as constant tension and the greatest systemic confrontation of ideas and states since the Reformation. This period endured the last wave of colonization during the 1920s and massive decolonization in the 1950s and 1960s. The physical, technological, political, and economic shrinkage of the globe made it impossible for nations to continue to pursue their own separate paths. Virtually all were caught in one or another cycle of violence even when they asked only to be left alone.

The dominant feature of the second half of the 75-year war was the nuclear confrontation, for the bipolar world of the cold war represented a combination of terror and control that was unprecedented in history. Two states, the United States and the Soviet Union, had the power and potentially the inclination to destroy each other and, indirectly, the entire world. Both knew the authority which that power gave them, but they also knew the responsibility. Each drew back from confrontations that might have forced them to unleash the power of the bomb, and each consciously included the thinking of the other in its own decision processes whenever such a confrontation approached. It was only when one or another made an unexpected move, as in the Cuban missile crisis of 1962, that the careful calculations on which they based their mutual deterrence risked unraveling.

Because of the immense awe in which both governments held their own power, they did not give others the authority to control it. The United States never yielded direction over its nuclear weapons to any other state or to any independent military command, although it gave others—including West Germany and now Germany—the opportunity to consult on nuclear deployment and usage. The Soviet Union acted with even greater caution. During the Cuban missile crisis of 1962, Moscow never permitted the Cuban government to decide what to do with the nuclear weapons that had been brought to the island. Information that has come out since the end of the Soviet Union has shown that this was a wise decision.

During the cold war, the most terrifying scenarios were considered, discussed, dissected, and rehearsed in the most precise, almost surgical, manner on both sides. The cold war became a modern version of a dance of death, in which the principals shared both common and opposing interests at different levels. This combination led to highly abstruse and even tortured calculations of balance and risk, leading both sides to increase their stockpiles to unimaginably high levels at the same time as they reinforced their precautions and intensified their negotiations in order to control the very weapons they were accumulating. Thus came the hydrogen bomb, the intercontinental missile, the plans for a Strategic Defense Initiative, unending arms control negotiations, and the hot line between Washington and Moscow.

Germany and Europe lay at the center of the nuclear confrontation. The fulcrum of the balance of power lay on European, and specifically German, soil. If the Soviet Union could have conquered or gained control over all of Germany, the position of the global concert in Europe would have been hopelessly compromised and Moscow would have won the cold war. The stakes were enormous for both sides, and they went far beyond Germany itself.

The danger was also great. Although the confrontations in Korea, Cuba, and Indochina had shown that the major powers were not prepared to risk nuclear war for small stakes, it seemed quite possible that they would be prepared to risk it for the sake of the European balance. The Western powers could not be sure whether the Soviet Union would risk a nuclear war in order to conquer Germany and win Europe, but they believed that the Soviet Union would certainly attack if the West was not prepared to risk war in turn. They concluded that the only way to deter war in Europe was to let Moscow know in advance that such a war might well be nuclear.

The members of the NATO alliance therefore agreed that they would be ready to fight a nuclear war in Europe if necessary. The West German government joined in this agreement because it wanted to deter war. It even participated in designing scenarios for nuclear use. This was a macabre scenario, the final curse that Hitler had placed on the German people. The German nation had to contemplate destroying itself in order to prevent attack, and Germans had to prepare to fight precisely the kind of war they did not want to fight. Germany's readiness to endure that risk was its main contribution to the European confrontation between the global concert and the Communist empire.

Americans engaged in the same kind of fearsome calculations. To deter a potential Soviet attack across the inner-German border, the United States had to threaten retaliation against Soviet territory itself, and it had to threaten to strike Soviet territory with intercontinental missiles and aircraft from the United States as well as with weapons positioned in Europe. American territory would be as much at risk as German territory. Americans would die to defend Germans whom they had only recently fought. Many Americans felt as uncomfortable with that proposition as Germans felt about the risk to Germany, but each believed that only the clearly articulated determination to make such a sacrifice would deter a possible Soviet attack.

The scenarios were never tested. The attack did not come. Even during the most acute phase of the Berlin Wall crisis of 1961–1962, neither the Soviet Union nor the NATO powers ever acted in ways that might have provoked nuclear war. The Soviet moves against Berlin were carefully calculated to avoid a clash. When the Soviets blocked Checkpoint Charlie at the Friedrichstrasse crossing between West and East Berlin, they always permitted some forms of traffic to pass. When they blocked civilian access to Berlin, they still permitted military convoys and flights to continue. The tanks of both superpowers withdrew in even measure from the Checkpoint Charlie confrontation in the fall of 1961. Soviet actions always fell short of the kind of provocations that might have brought on a war.

The Wall itself was carefully presented as a defensive measure. It was introduced in ways that made it difficult for the Western allies to react sharply. The Soviet and East German authorities may even have had reason to believe that it would not lead to a nuclear engagement, for authoritative American figures like Senator William Fulbright had signalled that the United States would not object to steps that Moscow took to control its own occupation areas.

During the entire cold war confrontation over Germany and Europe, every political leader and strategic planner kept the importance of strict control over nuclear weapons clearly in mind. They designed their war and escalation scenarios on the basis of the assumption that they faced a rational adversary who was making careful and even conservative calculations of potential profit and loss.

Except for some uncertainty about Premier Nikita Khrushchev, who was perceived as dangerously unpredictable, the West appeared confident that it could
decide its own course based on a fairly good understanding of what the adversary
might do or not do. Even East German dictator Walter Ulbricht was not regarded
as irrational, although Western planners believed that he was ready to take greater
risks than Khrushchev or other Russian leaders might be prepared to take.

With the ending of the cold war and the disintegration of the Soviet Union,
this calculation has to reevaluated. The nuclear weapons remain, but the central
controls over them have weakened; and the thinking of the new leaders in the
Commonwealth of Independent States (CIS) is not clearly understood. Few
Westerners really know the new leaders in all the republics, including those that
have nuclear weapons on their territories, and few of those leaders know the West.
They do, however, understand that access to those weapons remains a powerful
interest for their new states, although there is no reason to expect that any of the
new states might use nuclear weapons or any weapons of mass destruction. But
the West cannot have absolute confidence that current control mechanisms will
prevent any kind of unauthorized use. Nor can Western leaders be certain that
there will be no leaders who might be tempted to use nuclear weapons because
they believe that they have little to lose. Thus, even if there is less tension and less
risk of a global conflict, there is a greater risk of war by miscalculation at the edge
of Europe.

Outside Europe, the risk of major war has diminished. Those conflicts that
have been fomented or exploited by the great powers against each other, or those
in which the great powers have become reluctantly involved, have either been settled or appear to be on their way to settlement. The great powers have even helped
negotiate peace agreements, as in Afghanistan and Cambodia. But the risk of
conflict has not been eliminated. Dozens of insurgencies, civil wars, or ethnic
conflicts continue at one or another level of intensity. In the Middle East, not far
from the southern edge of Europe, tensions between Muslim fundamentalists
and the traditionalist regimes are mounting, and the talks between Israel and the
Palestinians remain inconclusive.

Instability and the potential for conflict are not new. They existed before the
twentieth century and they will outlive it. But what has been added is the risk that
some of those conflicts could now be nuclear, and that those nuclear weapons
would not be as rigorously controlled as those of the superpowers during the cold
war. Thus, although the ideological threats of the cold war have been removed,
the world that succeeds it is neither stable, peaceful, nor free of nuclear risk. For
the nuclear weapons cannot be wished away. The proliferation of weapons of
mass destruction remains a constant threat, and the ending of the cold war may
have released technicians who can help smaller states develop technologies that
earlier were the preserve of the superpowers. Thus, the nuclear danger is de-
creased in some ways but increased in others, leaving a lingering uncertainty.

The Soviet armed forces are scheduled to leave German territory before the end of 1994 and may leave even earlier, and the threat of Soviet military attack in Europe has faded; but the risk of some kind of unpredictable sequence of events leading to a nuclear detonation, even if not a full-scale nuclear war, has not been eliminated any more for Europe than for other parts of the world.

The collapse of the Soviet Union has posed one severe and unprecedented problem, the potential for nuclear wars as well as for nonnuclear crises within the former Communist imperium. It is the first time that a dying empire and its component states have had nuclear teeth, as well as the first time that so many deep problems have suddenly erupted after having been so long and so massively suppressed.

Any cursory glance at the history of revolution should warn us that the upheavals in Russia and in the other new republics are far from over. The risk of further revolutions remains, especially because of the economic and social crises that can be expected to come. Civil wars already rage in several of the newly autonomous republics. Some of the republics have begun to fight each other, either for territorial or for ethnic reasons, and the threat of conflict even between the Ukraine and Russia has been very real on several occasions during 1992. The Russian lands and their surroundings were not stable before the Russian revolution, and there is little reason to be confident that they will be stable now. And the consequences of major upheaval in any of the republics could have global consequences, especially as nuclear powers could be involved on both sides.

Even as these risks remain, however, the world is slowly turning its attention to other matters that now seem more urgent than the potential for political and military crisis. Those matters can be described under the broad rubric of economic development. They include the desire of the third world for greater economic and social progress, global environmental concern, the persistent global refugee crisis, new and old global diseases such as AIDS and the revival of malaria, and the risk of explosive population growth. They also include the risk of resource conflicts, like the Iraqi invasion of Kuwait followed by the Gulf War of 1991.

Some of these concerns, especially the drive for rapid economic development, have seized the former Communist states. The people and their new political leaders are demanding economic development as their first priority. These demands can help stabilize international affairs, at least in the short run, because they may compel governments to concentrate their energies on solving economic problems rather than engaging in political threats or military campaigns.

There are, however, two potential risks associated with the pressure for urgent development. The first is that governments that find themselves unable to guarantee economic progress will foment political crises in order to keep themselves in power. The other is that populations that fail to advance fast enough will become alienated and restive, beginning another cycle of revolution.

These dangers place a special burden on the global concert. A broad consensus in Eastern Europe and the CIS now supports the Western economic model. The concert hopes for Western investment, Western-type consumer goods, and

Western styles in management. It expects these Western models to bring about rapid progress and prosperity. But when that progress comes only haltingly, and when prosperity comes more slowly than expected, the risk of disappointment is all the greater.

The states of the G-7, as the governing board of the world, have to find ways to mobilize and coordinate their resources to help simultaneously in all corners of the globe, with each corner having different problems, different needs, and different dangers if the process fails.

It is a cold and wary peace the world now enters, not a warm and comfortable one. But it is still a peace. It must be greeted as such, and the various opportunities and pressures that it creates warrant examination. In particular, one must examine the impact of the new world on Europe and on two of the closest cold war allies, the United States and Germany.

4

THE NEW EUROPE

Europe is no longer divided. It is whole and free. It is no longer a prize to be won by others. Instead, it is again a major player in its own right. It will set its own future and help determine the state and the future of the world. Europe can be a new and more important element in the trans-Atlantic relationship, and it may even be able to function as a powerful new partner in the global concert.

The great European decline, which began in 1914 and was in many ways self-imposed, has now ended. The continent is again at peace and united. It is, however, potentially unstable again.

The new Europe will play a determining role in German-American relations. For a German chancellor and a German nation must see a different Europe from the one they saw before, and those changes in Europe are much more important than the changes in the world as a whole.

Even if Europe is politically free and no longer divided by a military border, it nonetheless remains divided by another border that may take longer to remove. That border represents a development gap that will not be completely closed for decades or longer, even if the process of closing it has already begun.

Europe is half rich and half poor. Although the physical wall is down, the social and economic gap between Western and Eastern Europe is as great as it was at the fall of ancient Rome. The Eastern standard of living and the Eastern level of development lag far behind the West, and the gap can become insurmountable if there is no determined effort to close it. The public and private facilities that are taken for granted in the West, the personal possessions and the ease of existence, are part of a world that is completely different from that which exists in Central and Eastern Europe. The gap that had been modest in 1914, when World War I began, has turned into a chasm.

That gap exists not only in such overt and evident possessions as cars, refrigerators, television sets, etc. but in property in its widest sense. Many persons in the West own their homes, perhaps some vacation property, savings accounts, securities, assets to leave their children. Persons in the East do not own such things and cannot count on owning them at any significant level for many years. Wealth did not exist under the communist system. Capital in all its forms, therefore, must at first come from abroad, in the form of loans or investments, and it will be a long time before persons in Eastern European states can truly say that they are fully in control of a major portion of the productive facilities of their own countries. Eastern Europe is in a postcolonial situation and should be regarded as a post-colonial area. It has been under colonial rule. In the East European states, as in other colonial areas, industrial and agricultural development, like trade links, have been directed by foreign-imposed political considerations, not by the laws of economics. Many industries must be abandoned, and many economic activities have to be reshaped. Most serious, and most troubling, the costs of colonialism will remain for years.

Europe cannot remain split by an economic wall. It would collapse into anarchy in the East and panic about refugees in the West. The West Europeans have recognized this and have chosen to use economic aid as the best instrument available to prevent postcolonial political instability. But the amount of aid, and the time during which it will be needed, depend on the speed with which the East European states are able to raise themselves.

New lines are beginning to run across the European continent and across the continental division as Western aid and investment begin to flow and as the cold war barriers break down. The new lines are harder to see than the old lines, which were very obvious, but they offer the potential to bring the continent together again.

The old lines across Europe were vertical, running from north to south and splitting Eastern from Western Europe. They could be easily seen along the Berlin Wall, along the border between the Germanies, and along the armed frontier between the NATO and the Warsaw Pact countries. They ran along political and military borders and could be recognized instantaneously on a map because they were usually drawn in heavy ink and had different colors on either side. They still remain in social and economic terms, but they are less absolute than before.

The new lines do not run vertically, they run horizontally. They run from west to east, not from north to south. They are not marked in heavy print. They are too wide and too blurred for that. But they can become even more important than the old lines were because they can shape the new Europe and can help shape the new Western world. The new lines do not follow borders but cross them. Over time, they could make borders not only transparent but irrelevant.

The main east-west line, crossing the center of Europe in a broad sweep, runs from western Germany to Russia across eastern Germany, Poland, and Belarus. On the way, it touches Hungary, the new Czech Republic, Slovakia, and the Ukraine. Germany will give the states of the former Soviet Union about DM 70 billion in aid and credits over the next several years and will give the states of Eastern Europe about DM 40 billion. Investment, joint ventures, and trade are to flow along those lines in order to help close the gap between the different parts of Europe.

But Germany is not the only West European state to open new avenues to the East. Austria is racing to reestablish old links with Hungary, the Czech Republic,

Slovakia, Slovenia, and now Croatia. It is also making agreements with the Ukraine, setting up joint ventures, aid programs, and other commercial and tourist routes. Italy is becoming active in Eastern Europe, especially in Albania but also in other parts of former Yugoslavia. France and Great Britain are also moving into the CIS and Eastern Europe with trade and investment. Even Americans, although far away, are investing heavily in Central and Eastern Europe.

Turkey, for its part, is opening relations with the Muslim states in the southern parts of the Commonwealth of Independent States. It is not only sending money but teachers, engineers, and technicians. It is now the most modernized and Westernized Muslim state and it is trying to establish a presence before those states turn to the fundamentalist states south of the CIS such as Iran and perhaps Afghanistan.

In Northern Europe, new lines are also opening, but they move northeast as well as directly east. Germany, Denmark, Sweden, and Finland are building new trade and investment links to the Baltic states of Estonia, Latvia, and Lithuania. They are opening embassies, consulates, trade missions, and travel bureaus. They are also moving into St. Petersburg.

The Baltic has changed dramatically since 1989. It no longer teems with spy submarines nosing into Western and neutral waters but with trade, tourism, and all the many forms of contact that flowed across it even before the Vikings. In several years, the states that border on the Baltic will have drawn together in commercial and production patterns that will create a powerful Baltic consciousness and perhaps common Baltic political and economic associations.

One additional step still must follow, however. The West must ultimately help not only by offering aid but by actually permitting low-cost products from Eastern Europe to compete in Western Europe. Even if most East European products cannot compete in Western Europe, the East will soon have a comparative advantage in agricultural goods, textiles, and basic industrial products such as steel. Those goods were traditionally exported from Eastern to Western Europe, from what is now Poland and Hungary as well as from other countries. But they are now produced in the West, often subsidized, and the West European states have not yet been ready to close their own production lines or farms in order to buy lower-cost products from Eastern Europe.

The dilemma is easy to state economically but difficult to accept politically: If Western Europe wishes the East European states to be truly prosperous, it must also be prepared to buy from them and not only to send them aid. Only by importing products from East European states will the West enable the East to accumulate its own capital and to become a true equal. Otherwise, aid may be permanently needed—with all that this implies in political as well as economic terms.

As these new lines across Europe become more important, as a new European consciousness begins to arise, and as decisions about aid or trade need to be made, the development of European organizations will become increasingly important. For the lines that run across Europe will force changes in all the institutions built during divided Europe. The lines represent realities that are too powerful to be ignored. They represent some of the most important natural lines of the continent, of its people and its resources, and they will sooner or later make themselves felt in politics, economics, and defense.

Most of the organizations in Europe were originally established for Western Europe. Those were established by Moscow for Eastern Europe, such as the Warsaw Pact and the Council for Mutual Economic Assistance (CMEA), have ceased to exist. Instead, the East European states are now trying to join such Western organizations as the European Community (EC) and the North Atlantic Treaty Organization (NATO).

One major international organization covers the continent from east to west and also includes the United States and Canada. It is the Conference for Security and Cooperation in Europe (CSCE), established in Helsinki in 1975. It has a consultative security function as well as economic and human rights functions, and it has been widely praised as the institution that helped bring freedom to Eastern Europe by providing a legal basis for widespread demands for human rights. With the disappearance of the Iron Curtain, that organization has assumed greater responsibilities, and even Japan now wants to join it.

The European Community is, however, of greater immediate interest to many East Europeans. They want to use the Community to link their economies with those of Western Europe. They hope that this will bring progress at home and also open more avenues for trade with the West as a whole and especially with Western Europe.

The EC itself, however, is changing at the same time. At the Maastricht summit of EC chiefs of state and government in December, 1991, the Community chose to create a closer monetary and political union for its present members. Its leaders decided to move toward European Monetary Union (EMU) with a single European currency by 1997 if enough states meet certain monetary and fiscal convergence requirements, or by 1999 for those that qualify. They also agreed at Maastricht to coordinate their foreign policies more closely. Even if the terms of the Maastricht agreement are not finally accepted in their entirety by all EC members, the directions in which the agreement points will continue to exert a great pull on all Europeans.

The EC has agreed to join in a closer union with the states of the European Free Trade Association (EFTA), forming a combined area of almost 400 million persons as the European Economic Area (EEA). Such states as Sweden, Norway, Austria, and Switzerland would then become more closely associated with the EC, accepting EC rules and regulations and establishing common trading practices toward the outside world. Some may even join the EC as separate members during the next several years.

The Maastricht summit and the formation of the EEA could complicate the expansion of the European Community toward Eastern Europe. Although Hungary and Poland have already applied for entry to the EC, many economists have questioned whether it would be possible for the Community to integrate more deeply in Western Europe and simultaneously permit new members from Central and Eastern Europe. If the integration process in Western Europe moves too fast, no East European state may be able to qualify for entry. But if the EC postpones integration in order to wait for East European states, it may miss a historic opportunity.

Despite these difficulties, it now seems likely that at least one or two of the Central and East European applicants will be accepted into the EC before the end of the century, although the exact terms and dates have yet to be negotiated. Several Baltic states might also want to apply for membership, as might Belarus, the Ukraine, and perhaps Russia and other East European states. The European Community could become a truly pan-European integrating force, linking all of Europe into a single market and a single economic entity.

But other forces, more worrisome, are also at work in Europe. For if the continent is half rich and half poor, it is also half stable and half unstable, and some of the instability could flow from east to west. It is riven with potentially severe fissures and risks. A reversal toward Russian militarism (Chapter 3) would hurt Europe (and Germany) more than any other area. The disintegration of Yugoslavia and the division of Czechoslovakia have also raised an ancient specter that has long haunted Europe: ethnic strife and nationalist rivalry spreading outward from the Balkans and also drawing other powers into the morass of that long-standing center of ethnic and religious strife. Virtually every European state has at least one and sometimes more significant groups of ethnic minorities, and any hint of revived European ethnic strife could generate massive chaos.

As one contemplates the new Europe after the cold war, one cannot help but ask if it is perhaps not really a new Europe but an old one, the Europe before 1914. In many ways, that is correct. For, like the Europe before 1914, the new Europe is not militarily divided between East and West. One can even perceive the dawning of a spirit of cultural unity that parallels Europe before 1914, and the continent can again over time acquire the kind of cultural cohesion that it enjoyed before 1914. More important, Europe is now evolving in directions that could undo at least some of the results of the Versailles and Yalta settlements.

Most worrisome, of course, is that Europe before 1914 was not an area of stability but of instability. European states fought each other, sometimes on their own continent and sometimes on other continents. They aligned and realigned continually in political patterns that tested the wits of countless statesmen and that killed countless soldiers and civilians. The prospect of a return to the Europe before 1914 cannot be contemplated with equanimity either by Americans or by Europeans themselves.

The differences, however, outnumber the parallels, and they are generally encouraging. The Europe of 1992 is not split between competing alliance systems, as the Europe before 1914 often was. It has no major irredentist powers seeking revenge, like France before 1914 (or Germany after 1919). It also has a number of supranational structures that give it a sense of cohesion and common identity that it did not have in 1914. Thus, despite the social and economic gap, there can be a real peace in Europe if nations and statesmen are determined to keep that peace.

The most important feature of the new Europe may, however, be its intense concentration upon itself and upon its own problems. Unlike during the nineteenth and early twentieth centuries, when European states were looking for colonial adventure and foreign rivalry, they are now working to build their own countries and their own continent. They want to avoid rather than to find international adventure. The Europe of the 1990s must deal primarily with its own problems, its own search for identity, and its own organization and development, even as it decides its future.

The new Europe also has an American presence, which it did not have before 1914. That presence was a vital element in the preservation of Western Europe's freedom and in the restoration of Eastern Europe's. It was also the basic element in the protective presence of the global concert. But one must ask if that presence is now still needed or whether it is still wanted, by the Europeans or the Americans, in this new world and new Europe.

Europe is poised uncertainly between the nineteenth and the twenty-first centuries, having to choose between a return to the nationalist and separatist ethic that marked the continent before 1914 and an advance into a wider community. It is uncertain whether America has a role to play in this evolution. Some Europeans might argue that a European identity must be part of a European community, and that such an identity can only be established if American power and influence are excluded from the continent. But the American presence after World War II point helped to promote European cooperation by making it easier for Europeans to associate with each other without having to concern themselves with relative standing and authority.

Americans, like Europeans, now wonder how the transatlantic link should now evolve.

One must therefore examine the role and the attitudes of Americans in the new world, as one examines the attitudes of Europeans.

One must also particularly examine the role and the attitudes of Germany. For it was Germany's defeat and division that brought America to Europe, and it was the association between those two states that most definitively shaped Europe and the world during the past forty years.

5

THE NEW GERMANY

Germany, suddenly united, is facing immense difficulties not only in completing its own unification but also in defining its new European and global role. Those difficulties will continue well into the next century. German domestic attitudes about foreign policy remain confused, as do foreign attitudes about a more powerful German role.

Germany's unification, a moment of triumph, is thus also a moment of doubt, for Germany and its allies.

For the new Germany must do what a united Germany has twice before failed to do: find a role and a direction that give free rein to the energies, the talents, and the wishes of the German people as well as to the power of the German state, and that are nonetheless also acceptable to others. And it must find that role and that direction not only in Europe but in the world as a whole. This search will constitute one of the major tests of German and global statesmanship.

Germany was divided between hundreds of different and often competing sovereignties during most of its history. Many German monarchies, principalities, dukedoms, and ecclesiastical states fought each other for centuries as bitterly as they might have fought other nations. They developed no lasting legacies regarding common policies or common attitudes.

German land and people were governed or contested by other states for centuries. Unlike Great Britain or France, or even the more distant United States, the geographic and ethnic entity that has come to be known as Germany has no centuries-old tradition of foreign policy and no sense of long-established interests. Germany developed no widely accepted consensus about what should be the foreign policy that would most closely conform to its basic interests.

When Germany was united in 1871, its leaders regarded their country as a regional player within Europe rather than as a global power. Its first emperor, Wilhelm I, and his first chancellor, Otto von Bismarck, were far more successful in a regional role than Emperor Wilhelm II was when he sought a German "place in the sun" around the world. Many Germans learned from that experience that Europe was a more congenial and more appropriate arena than the world as a whole. The Weimar Republic acted accordingly during the 1920s. The results of Germany's experience under Adolf Hitler not only reinforced the lesson but drove it home to stay.

At the *Stunde Null,* the "zero hour" of German capitulation in 1945, there was no compass to guide a new German foreign policy except an absolute and widespread determination to avoid repeating what had gone before. One could not then be fully certain what the lessons of history might be for Germany, but the dominant themes were hesitation born of uncertainty and disgrace and the search for legitimation by alliances with respected other states.

At this deepest point in its history, West Germany came to rely primarily on the United States and to a lesser degree on the other Western allies, not only for support and guidance in reorganizing itself but also for the defense of its military and political interests. And the Americans responded by playing the principal role in the creation and defense of the new West German state.

American political scientists, many of them refugees from Germany, such as Carl Friedrich, helped to draft the new German Basic Law. The new German central bank, the Bundesbank, was modeled on the U.S. Federal Reserve Bank. The first leaders of the Federal Republic of Germany were either selected by American occupation officials or approved by them, sometimes against the wishes of other occupying powers. Ludwig Erhard, the founder of the German "economic miracle," used to say that he was an American invention. Konrad Adenauer and his policy of firm links to the Western powers had the determined support of the United States because the U.S. government feared that a neutral Germany could not remain free in the shadow of the Soviet Union.

The United States also shaped the foreign security arrangements of the new West Germany. It not only established and sustained the strategic balance with the Soviet Union but it created, organized, and commanded the main structures of the alliance. America had the nuclear forces, the blue-water navy, the worldwide system of bases, and the intercontinental bombers and missiles that could deter war. It also retained the political respect and attention that Germany—and the German people—had surrendered.

Over time, and with the help of others such as France, Italy, and Great Britain, West Germany came to again play a major role in Europe.

- West German forces, with the agreement of Germany's allies, constituted the largest national contingent of NATO's conventional forces. West Germany served as the main base for American conventional forces, especially after France withdrew from the NATO integrated command and expelled U.S. forces from its territory. West Germany also permitted the United States to station the nuclear devices and the delivery systems that helped deter a European war, although it recognized the particular risks that the presence of those forces posed. When the European balance was threatened, as it was during the late 1970s when the Soviet Union deployed the SS-20 missiles, West German leaders not only called attention to the threat but helped correct the imbalance despite domestic protests that brought down one German government and tried to bring down another.

- West Germany immersed itself in Western Europe and especially in the European Community. West German political and economic leaders constantly visited Brussels and other European capitals. As German influence grew, German views increasingly carried the day in many intra-European discussions. Germans also financed the largest single portion of the EC budget. Half of all West German trade was with other EC states, and three quarters of it was within Europe. West German monetary influence came to dominate Europe, and it played a fundamental role in the arrangements agreed on at Maastricht, although it did so because of the policies that the German government and the Bundesbank pursued at home rather than because Germany wanted to establish any particular kind of European regime.
- The most difficult task was German reconciliation with Central and Eastern Europe, especially in areas where the Nazi armies had been particularly brutal in their occupation policies. West Germany tried to overcome those memories by practicing accommodation, reconciliation, and the slow but steady development of economic and political links. Under the policy that came to be known as *Ostpolitik,* West Germany signed treaties with the Soviet Union, with East Germany, and with the Central and East European states under Soviet domination. The states in the East did not forget the Nazi occupation. While welcoming greater contacts, they kept them under tight control. The U.S. government approved the steps toward German reconciliation with the Soviet Union, but only after some hesitation. It feared an independent German approach to Moscow, evoking the memory of the Rapallo Treaty of 1922.

Many Germans have drawn a clear and simple lesson from their historical experience as well as from their experience during the cold war: Germany can play a useful role and can even achieve something in Europe, but it should never again try for a wider political or military reach. Many Germans firmly believe that they must never take a global path again, and they react very skeptically to any suggestion that they should do so. There are no positive recollections in German history to justify a global policy. No German government can now want to pursue such a policy.

There are, moreover, many reasons for Germany to feel comfortable in Europe. West Germany and now united Germany can find in Europe an arena that matches German interests, capacities, and influence. German experience in Europe, even in the recent past, reinforces the belief that this is an appropriate and useful area for the exercise of German policy.

History imposes some limits on Germany even in the European context. A number of Europeans were quite apprehensive about the resurgence of German military power, even within NATO, and they accepted it only because it was necessary and because the West German government imposed some far-reaching limitations on the deployment of its forces. Despite the experience of dealing with West Germany, a number of European states were uncomfortable at the prospect of German unification and would perhaps not have accepted it if the United States had not supported it so strongly. They look even more nervously at German weight and German power when Germany is united than when it was divided.

Paradoxically, a divided Germany could express its interests and its views more freely without arousing fear or suspicion than a united Germany can. And many Europeans, including many Germans, want the United States to remain firmly committed to Europe because they want to avoid German domination. They also want the United States to continue to maintain European stability, as well as global stability, in order to avoid the resurgence of intra-European rivalries.

During the cold war, the global concert offered West Germany military protection and political acceptance and support, solving the two most important problems faced by the new German state. It embraced and sheltered those parts of Germany that were occupied by the Western states, including West Berlin. The West Germans and the Berliners in turn helped preserve and protect the global system. The Germans, and especially the Berliners, legitimized the presence of the global concert in central Europe. They gave the maritime powers the necessary strategic foothold on the Eurasian continent. They welcomed and supported the system's ideals of democracy and free markets. They also anchored the eastern end of the American alliance system, making it possible for the global concert to become a truly international force that reached across three continents and that could over time determine the future of the world.

West Germany functioned comfortably and effectively within the Western system and within its global reach. As American power became less monolithic, Germany became a founding member of the system's governing board, the Group of Seven. It participated with growing weight in major international strategic and financial decisions, sharing most of the risks and burdens as well as most of the benefits. It had a secure and respected role at the core of the system, although it was geographically on the periphery. It grew to power, influence, and acceptance. It was not fully sovereign, but it was stable and its policies were effective.

When the Soviet imperium collapsed, the West Germans could rightfully claim to have played an important and even crucial role in the victory of the global concert system and of the Western powers. Their reward was unification, not only for Germany but also for Europe. This gave Germany a greater influence as well as a greater arena. It shifted Berlin back from the rim to the center and has given it an opportunity once again to become the future capital of united Europe in all but name. The history that was arrested in 1914 can now continue, hopefully in a better direction.

United Germany is a different creature from West Germany. It has different boundaries, different neighbors, different interests, different priorities, different politics, and a different weight. It is fully sovereign. It will, and even must, pursue

policies that will be different from West Germany's. It will have a greater consciousness of its own independent role and interests than West Germany had. As
the Federal Republic of Germany, it may have the same official name as the
former West Germany, but it is not the same entity.

Germany will, and even must, see the world differently than does the global
concert's leader, the United States. In political and strategic terms, Germany is a
European continental power, not a global one. But in economic—and especially
in monetary—terms, it has a global reach.

Germany did not send forces to the Gulf War despite strong U.S. entreaties,
although it contributed funds. Germany recognized Slovenia and Croatia in the
Yugoslav civil war, despite objections from its allies in Europe and America. In
both instances, it followed its own distinct course, and it disturbed other important states.

Matters like the Gulf and Yugoslavia, however, pale into insignificance before
the major tasks that Germany must now undertake if it wishes to preserve the
global system and the global concert, tasks it must accomplish without again
arousing the old questions about Germany's role and purpose in the world order.
Those tasks are not imposed by Germany's allies, and they may not even be fully
understood by its people, but they are imposed by German interests in the new
European and global arena.

- The first task is to serve as the link between Western Europe and the Atlantic
  states, keeping an integrating Western Europe within the global concert even
  as both Europe and the global concert evolve.
- The second task is to serve as the link between the entire Western system and
  the East, trying to help bring the alienated and eviscerated victims of the
  Leninist-Stalinist tyranny into a pan-European and ultimately into a global
  system.
- The third task, and the most important as well as most sensitive, is to help to
  reshape the global concert itself in order to adjust it to the world's new realities of power and to the world's new types of security needs.

In its first task, linking the integrating European Community and the Atlantic
system, the crucial element for Germany will be the influence that it can bring to
bear on French, British, and American policies.

Charles de Gaulle, like Napoleon, wanted to create a continental order that would
be independent of the maritime powers (whom he termed the Anglo-Saxons). Even
after de Gaulle, French leaders feel more comfortable in a European than in an
Atlantic system, and they constantly strive to establish continental arrangements that
will supplant, supplement, or parallel the global and Atlantic order.

West Germany would not and could not join de Gaulle's challenge to the maritime powers because only the transatlantic guarantee could protect its freedom
and independence. A united Germany, however, facing a divided and impotent

East, may no longer need as much transatlantic protection. It could, perhaps, try to give greater weight to its European vocation even if it would still need some link to the maritime powers for contingency protection and for economic reasons. Many recent German policies suggest that the German government is weighing and perhaps following that option.

The Atlantic maritime powers of the global concert question and even oppose separate continental strategic and economic structures. They have made their preferences for transatlantic systems clear.

Germany now sits at the center of all the new east-west lines that run across Europe. It is the only state that has the power to create an arrangement that will resolve the differences between the maritime and the continental powers. It has not yet shown conclusively how it will try to balance its integration into an ever tighter Europe with its position in the transatlantic (and global) system—and whether it will even try to keep the United States, Great Britain, and France together. It may be prepared to let the maritime powers withdraw from continental Europe. The choice it makes may not be the one that the United States may wish it to make.

Germany's second task will be the integration of the East into the West and into the world system.

One of the reasons for the success and durability of the Western system has been its readiness on most occasions to incorporate and adopt those whom it has defeated, or at least to find a place for them. In accordance with this tradition, the West European and the Atlantic states have already moved toward new links with the states of Central and Eastern Europe, and they are also beginning to reach out to the newly established (or reestablished) states of the former Soviet Union and especially to Russia.

Among European and even Atlantic states, only Germany now has the available resources that can make the transformation of Eastern Europe and the former Soviet Union succeed. Only Germany can provide enough capital, enough know-how, and perhaps enough of a market to make a genuine difference. It also has the strongest interest in establishing successful links between East and West. It must be the principal Western agent to the East, and also the principal Eastern agent in the West.

Germany is beginning to engage in the second task, although not without some hesitation because of its potentially unlimited cost. But the magnitude of the task will grow, and even German resources will need to be substantially augmented by other members of the global system. Generating enough aid and coordinating Western policies and programs will require enormous dedication, a long-term commitment, some forbearance on all sides, and a readiness to persist despite intermittent upheavals.

Although the states of the West should and will welcome Germany's commitment, it is not certain that they will do what the Germans will expect of them. They may accuse Germany of having returned to its old Eastern vocation and of having abandoned the West once again for another try at a Rapallo system. They may also be unready to make the concessions that would permit truly free trade between Eastern and Western Europe.

The most delicate and important task for Germany lies in helping to reshape the global concert system itself. For despite frequent references to the United States as being the only remaining superpower, Americans now must share leadership of the world even more than before with others. Among those are their friends and rivals Germany and Japan, who do not fully agree with all American attitudes and policies.

Through their direct talks and through the Group of Seven, the Germans as well as the Japanese and the Americans have to begin to define a new arrangement of power within the global order. All want to preserve that order, but each will also want to adjust it to suit individual interests and preferences. The Group of Seven needs to be reinvigorated in order to take its place in the new world and in order to take on its new responsibilities within that world, and Germany can play the key role in that reinvigoration, not only through the government but also through the Bundesbank.

In at least two areas, any German government will want to pursue a distinct path that will not be the same as that normally followed by the United States.

One area is diplomacy. The Germans have long believed that "security" policy means not only military force but also diplomatic instruments. They will try to move the alliance toward flexible diplomatic arrangements to supplement at least some of the current military structures, even if they want the structures to remain. They may attempt this on a global as well as a continental basis. They can be expected to look for a new and more flexible security architecture with newer as well as older partners.

Another area is money. The Germans have usually pursued a much stricter monetary policy than has the United States. They are now imposing that policy on Europe, not without some negative as well as positive effects, through the 1997–1999 convergence requirements of the impending European Monetary Union and through the policies of the Bundesbank after unification. Once that policy is imposed on Europe, it can be expected to carry a new weight and perhaps even to impose itself globally. This will have an effect in the United States as well as elsewhere, for it will introduce a powerful new disinflationary—and perhaps even deflationary—force into the global monetary system as a whole. The effect in Europe may give some indication of what the global effect might be.

As these German ideas and attitudes begin to prevail, perhaps in conjunction with Japan's, the global concert itself must change in ways that cannot yet be fully foreseen. Those changes will be political, military, and economic. They will reflect not only the collapse of the Soviet empire but the shift in the leadership of the global system itself.

The dilemma that Germany will have to resolve is how to join the united Europe and the global order without changing either so much that the system cannot function. It must also maintain its own position both in Europe and in the global order, keeping contact with Washington and the principal European capitals. Some American or Japanese approaches may have to be kept, especially with respect to the global trading system. But Western Europe may have special wishes about a European security zone or a special European trading system. Those may not be compatible with American wishes and policies. Germany has the most important interest in preserving European and global cooperation, and the greatest incentive to make the system function.

Germany, whether it wishes or not, will thus have an important role to play in the shifting world order. For only Germany can link the global, European, and Eastern systems while remolding each. Ironically, the nation that was once a pariah may become an essential lynchpin for a new international combination of structures. It must serve as the principal agent of the global concert in Europe, and as the major agent of Europe within the global concert.

What will emerge, once the changes are in place and even as they are evolving, is an arrangement that will be different even if not completely new. The global system may, finally, have adjusted to German needs, just as Germany has adjusted to the system's requirements.

One must ask, however, whether every affected state, especially in the West, will accept such a powerful German role and mission. France and Britain—as well as other Europeans—may well question whether Germany should have the right to shape Europe. The United States itself has shown—especially during and after President George Bush's trip to Japan in early 1992—that it does not relish being eased out of its commanding position even if it does not want to pay the price to keep its place. Many states who welcome and even seek German support and resources are not ready to give Germany a much greater role.

The Atlantic states, and especially America, show ambivalence toward Germany. They want a strong and united Germany, but they react with considerable suspicion and even alarm to German policies that do not meet the postwar pattern. They subconsciously want a united Germany that will act as the former West Germany did, even if they are prepared to accept a more powerful Germany intellectually.

Many Germans, in turn, show similar ambivalence. They expect Americans and others to understand that Germany's new policies will not be identical to the old. But many Germans are not sure what new policies they want to follow. Nor do they know where they can compromise and where they cannot. Many Germans do not particularly want to play a global role or even a European one and are themselves uncertain how to react to new situations, new opportunities, and new risks.

Germany's leaders are very conscious of the past, when Germany reached too far too fast. They want to be careful not to repeat the mistakes of their predecessors, even as they also want to pursue their own policies. They move unevenly, sometimes too slowly and sometimes too fast for others. The others are quick to criticize and the Germans, quick to react.

Memories of Hitler still cast a deep shadow between the Germans and others. The ghosts of the Third Reich arise, sometimes unexpectedly, at critical moments.

When Germany recognized Slovenia and Croatia, the Western press recalled Hitler's occupation of Yugoslavia and drew unpleasant parallels. When East German right-wing groups, legitimized by their earlier opposition to the Communist state, marched and acted against immigrants, many Western media evoked images of Nazi racism and xenophobia. Whatever the German present may be, the German legacy has made Germany different in many ways from other states. Some of Germany's neighbors still shudder at the notion that German forces might burst outside their borders again, and German political extremism is not only a domestic issue.

Even Germans who question the wisdom of a wider role for their nation resent those accusations. They see their recognition of the Yugoslav breakaway states as an affirmation, not a denial, of the right of self-determination. They insist, correctly, that right-wing racism is not confined to Germany. They also point out, and accurately, that some of the most massive demonstrations in postwar German history have been those in late 1992 and early 1993 which protested against the right-wing groups and against the terror that those groups carried out against foreigners.

But the accusations do show that even a united and democratic Germany needs to be conscious of the many potential traps and barriers along its new path. They also reflect the paradox between the widespread wish that Germany should carry greater responsibility and the readiness to criticize Germany when it appears to take too strong a lead.

If Germany can succeed in merging the Atlantic and the continental systems, and if it can succeed in creating bridges to the East and in helping to revive and to democratize the states of the former Soviet Union, it will already have begun to reshape the global system. Its further proposals are more likely to be accepted. It will have won an honored place, having performed a historic mission that could not have been achieved by any other people or state.

The states of the West also have to recognize that Germany is doing what must be done, and what only Germany can do. They may need to give the Germans more authority and credibility than they have been accustomed to giving.

For the new Germany is truly different from the old. It is not as ambitious as the German empire before World War I, but neither is it as weak as the Weimar Republic after the war. The incendiary combination of the Prussian officer class, the Pomeranian landholders, and the Ruhr arms monopolists has been destroyed. The ring that Otto von Bismarck forged around Prussia and Germany by blood and iron was shattered by Hitler and Stalin, and Prussia no longer even exists. And the new Germany is looking for a role, not for a place in the sun or for dominion. But even a democratic German state will still want and even need to pursue its own interests as other democracies do.

Unification was not an end but a beginning, not the last step but the first. And the search that the new united Germany must now conduct for its role and direction within the global system will continue and evolve over many years and perhaps over many decades.

But unification also brought its own perils and its own costs. The process has proven brutally expensive, not only in economic terms but in its social and political ramifications. It has cost more than a hundred billion D-marks in 1991 and 1992 and will probably cost as much, or almost as much, in every year until the turn of the century. The German fiscal deficit has grown out of control. The Bundesbank has reacted by attempting to tighten the money supply to counter the fiscal deficit. This has created a sharp recession that will last into 1994. The tightened money supply has led to unemployment in Western Germany to levels not seen in over a decade, and it has raised unemployment in Eastern Germany that will be unacceptable over the decade. The recession has also diverted German resources toward its own problems at precisely the moment when they are most needed for Germany's international objectives.

One must ask, therefore, whether Germany is now up to the tasks that it will have to face. Since unification, the new Germany has been mainly preoccupied with itself. The government is now not concentrating on its European, let alone global, responsibilities, although it is still attempting to support the Maastricht agreement and attempting to move Western Europe toward fuller integration. But it has been slow to take steps that might help integrate Eastern European states and it has not concentrated on strengthening or maintaining the transatlantic links forged by West Germany, although it has made some effort to avoid their rupture.

Germany and the Germans had become so accustomed to living on the periphery, with certain important but still limited responsibilities, that they are still not certain how to cope with a return to the center of Europe and with a suddenly long list of obligations arising from that as well as from the global roles that others are anxious to assign them. They are uncertain what is best, and they cannot be expected to decide in a hurry.

Until the process of full unification is completed in Germany and Europe, and until Germany has shown its long-term purposes on the global scene, many questions will continue to be posed, many uncertainties will exist both within and outside Germany, and many doubts will arise. Moreover, many others will attempt to push the Germans in one direction or another before the Germans are really prepared to make their own decisions.

The process of Germany's accession to a greater role may, in fact, never really end. And every step will be carefully measured, studied, and analyzed—for Germany is what it is and was what it was.

If Germany's accession to a greater role is to succeed, however, it must contain a German-American element that is acceptable both in Germany and in the United States, and that is also accepted by the publics as well as by the governments.

For that, Germany must decide what its own European and global roles will be over the long run, and what role it still wishes to accord America. The United States must in turn decide how far it wishes to remain involved in Europe, and how it can devise a German policy that will be compatible with that level of involvement.

In that context, it is now necessary to look at the American side of the equation.

6

THE NEW AMERICA

The United States of America led the coalition that won the third great war of the twentieth century, the cold war, as it had led the coalitions that had won the first two great wars of the century. It carried the West and the global concert to a victory over the Communist system that had seized the Soviet Union and many other states and governments.

The cold war represented a new and different kind of struggle from the world wars. It was a war of armament, deployment, positioning, maneuver, posturing, and occasionally of actual battle, but the principals never fought each other directly. For the weapons in the hands of the principals were so powerful and so frightening that the leaders feared the weapons as much as they feared each other. The United States and the Soviet Union found other means to struggle, either through proxy wars, paramilitary conflicts, pressure tactics, propaganda, the creation and exploitation of different political and para-military groupings, satellite armies, and the dirty tricks of espionage, counterinsurgency, and covert action. This made the struggle longer and more widespread. Many observers were openly skeptical about America's ability to conduct and to sustain such a campaign, especially because constant arguments about strategy and tactics within the American government and in the American political and strategic establishment prevented the United States and its allies from fighting as the Soviet Union fought.

America was involved in conflict on every continent. Two major military engagements took place in Asia, with American ground forces committed to both. Several guerrilla wars were fought in Asia, Latin America, and Africa, with the Soviet Union and the United States supplying—and sometimes directing—the opposing parties. Political conflicts were fought in Europe as well as on other continents. Two dramatic and almost simultaneous confrontations occurred, over Cuba and over Berlin, but both protagonists were careful not to drive either confrontation to actual battle. It was a war with no respite, no safety zones, and no foreseeable ending, but with clearly identifiable limits and objectives.

The war strained American resources. Millions of men and women were kept under arms. An enormous navy and air force spanned the globe. Hundreds of thousands of troops were sent across the world, and many tens of thousands of lives were lost. Thousands of nuclear warheads were deployed in Europe as well as on U.S. aircraft, submarines, and missile bases. No comparable force had ever been assembled, trained, and deployed, and none may ever be again. In the confusion of the conflict, faced with the deceptive tactics of a totalitarian adversary and with drawn-out and seemingly endless tension, some Americans found it hard to tell friend from foe. There were others who blamed the entire conflict on the United States.

The Americans continually debated what should or should not be done. They argued about strategy, tactics, weapons, and force levels, confusing themselves, their allies, and sometimes perhaps even their enemies, but most Americans clearly believed that they had a moral as well as a political objective in fighting the war. It was this conviction, little understood abroad, that finally permitted the United States to prevail. The American body politic carried out the task better than most observers—including many Europeans—had expected, largely because it was able to hold a consensus together at home and throughout the entire alliance system. That consensus relied on common fear and a sense of common danger. Many states operated under that consensus and supported the American effort more than most Americans ever understood or appreciated. This was the foundation and the strength of the global concert, for America itself could not have fought as long or as successfully as it did if it had not had the support of its friends.

Now, the American consensus may well be in jeopardy. For as the American public passed through periods of great uncertainty after its two first victories of the twentieth century, it is now beginning again to question the purposes and the foundations of its foreign engagement. The American sense of moral mission has dissipated with the collapse of Communism. The United States left its continental preserve three times in order to defeat Kaiserism, Nazism, and Communism. The American people believed that they had been given historic tasks as "the arsenal of democracy" and "the leader of the free world." Having expended enormous effort to carry out those tasks, they want to shed their sense of mission and to pull back from their role. They also have come to regard many of their cold war allies as competitors in the now vital economic struggle and are, therefore, less inclined to support those allies as they did during the cold war.

American politicians and commentators, as well as the people at large, can now find little justification for an active American foreign policy. President George Bush's call for a "new world order" may have aroused some interest when it was first uttered in connection with the Gulf War, but the concept has never been fully articulated and debated in the American political process. It is neither widely understood nor widely accepted as a long-term guide to U.S. foreign policy. Bush has never thoroughly explained what the concept means to him.

The idea of a new world order contains several flaws that make it a poor long-term guide for U.S. foreign policy. It invites the United States to become either a world police power or a universal scold. The American public and its political leaders have long rejected and even derided such roles. Most Americans do not want to impose an order of their own on the world as a whole even if they do not like to have any other order imposed on them. The American people opposed the Nazis and the Communists largely because they feared that those systems were trying to establish world orders of their own. They would not want to be accused of the same thing.

Traditional and pragmatic arguments for foreign policy, such as the protection of U.S. national interests or the achievement of global prosperity, have never appealed to the American people as a long-term mission. Many Americans— including important political figures—now believe that the best way to protect U.S. interests is to cut back on foreign commitments, to husband American resources, and to reduce America's global role.

The notion of the United States as "sole remaining superpower," a concept that has attracted considerable comment and that is often repeated in the media, does not appeal to most Americans either. They do not know what it means to be such a superpower, and they do not know how they either can or should use whatever that power may represent.

The U.S. government and people thus find themselves without a moral justification or a domestic political base for an energetic global policy. They are also not at all certain that such a policy is needed. Therefore, unless there is a global crisis, America's role in the new world my remain in flux for several years with a general drift toward a lower level of involvement. On certain matters, as in its pursuit of the Gulf War or in its opposition to nuclear weapons proliferation, the United States may practice full engagement. Even those American politicians who have raised questions about the wisdom of an active U.S. foreign policy are prepared to insist on U.S. intervention in those world crises that affect their interests or their constituencies. But American policies are more likely to vacillate between commitment and withdrawal.

With the end of the cold war, the American public is readjusting its attitude toward foreign policy, and this is reflected in American politics. The 1992 election year was the first year since World War II in which foreign policy was not one of the most important questions on which voters chose a president:

- In 1948, Harry Truman was reelected on the basis of the Marshall Plan and of his measured but firm resistance to Communism in Europe.
- In 1952, Dwight Eisenhower was elected because of his promise to go to Korea in order to end the war.
- In 1956, President Eisenhower was reelected because he had ended the Korean War honorably but was also prepared to negotiate with the new Soviet leader, Nikita Khrushchev, in Geneva in 1955.
- In 1960, John Kennedy was elected because Americans feared that the Soviet Union was getting ahead in intercontinental nuclear weapons (the "missile gap").

- In 1964, President Lyndon Johnson was reelected because of fear that his opponent Barry Goldwater would be too unpredictable in foreign policy.
- In 1968, Richard Nixon was elected because of his promise to end the war in Vietnam.
- In 1972, President Nixon was reelected because of his visit to the People's Republic of China and because of his détente policy with the Soviet Union.
- In 1976, Jimmy Carter was elected because it appeared that détente had gone too far, especially in accepting Soviet domination over Eastern Europe.
- In 1980, Ronald Reagan was elected because Carter had been unable to solve the hostage crisis in Iran and appeared too weak in foreign affairs.
- In 1984, President Reagan was reelected because he seemed able to defend U.S. interests by an active foreign policy and arms acquisition policy.
- In 1988, George Bush was elected because, as Reagan's vice president, he was linked to Reagan's new détente with the Soviet Union.

There is no single pattern to these electoral victories. In some cases, the victors promised to be more compromising. In other cases, they promised to be less compromising. The American public wanted a president who could "stand up to the Russians," but not a president who would take the United States into long and costly commitments.

Uniformly, however, foreign policy had played a role in the elections before 1992. It may not have been the single most important issue in every election, although it played a decisive role in several, but it was always there and was always in the voters' minds. Domestic political and economic concerns were also important and sometimes decisive. But many voters made their choices on the basis of their analysis of how a potential or actual president would conduct, or had been conducting, the nation's foreign affairs.

This was not the case in 1992. Although there was some discussion of foreign affairs, all three of the presidential candidates stressed their ability to solve domestic problems and their ability to extricate the United States from foreign burdens. Other American politicians did the same. When President Bush asked for aid to Russia, the Congress linked it to domestic programs. The military budget is shaped much more than before by social considerations such as jobs in congressional districts than by the strategic requirements that used to be the dominant (if not exclusive) basis for decision.

Nor is the new American administration yet certain of its foreign policies. President Clinton focused his campaign primarily on domestic issues and even denounced Bush's foreign affairs experience as a sign that Bush was not attuned to America's real needs. Yet, in an inaugural address concentrated on domestic matters, he trumpeted an almost idealistic and interventionist global vision, asserting that America would act not only when its vital interests were challenged but also when the "will and conscience" of the international community were defied. It is not yet clear whether this statement should be dismissed as inaugural rhetoric or whether it represents Clinton's determination that America should maintain a global order of peace and justice that would transcend anything that any state has attempted to do in history. If the latter, the statement goes against not only the president's campaign promise to concentrate on the economy but also against the American people's preference for domestic affairs at this moment in their history. Perhaps in recognition of the current reluctance of Americans to become involved in costly international ventures, the president allowed for the possibility that America would act with diplomacy wherever possible and with force only when necessary.

American policy toward Europe will, like American global policy, remain in flux, especially as Europe reshapes itself along traditional lines. The United States never had a political and security role in historical Europe, although it had a very powerful and persistent interest in trading with Europe. Most Americans supported the European arrangements that emerged out of the peace treaties of Versailles and St. Germain after World War I, although the U.S. Senate did not approve the Treaty of Versailles because it included the League of Nations. However, most Americans opposed the Yalta and Potsdam arrangements because those agreements divided Europe, and most Americans supported a policy that kept Western Europe free and that linked it to the United States.

The end of European division means that Yalta and Potsdam have been superseded, which most Americans welcome. Nonetheless, neither the American public nor the U.S. Congress will want to extend to Eastern Europe or to the CIS states the kinds of commitments they were prepared to make to West European states. If the disintegration of Yugoslavia were to initiate a revision of the World War I treaty system throughout Central and Eastern Europe, the American public might be disturbed, but not enough to become actively engaged (except perhaps to help Poland). If Russia and the Ukraine were to go to war or to threaten each other, most Americans would regard it as a distant quarrel. They would support U.N. mediation and perhaps some efforts at conciliation, especially if there was any major risk that nuclear weapons might be used by either side, but they would not want to make a commitment to become engaged militarily in support of either party.

This cautious American attitude remained evident, if indirectly, during the crisis that followed the break-up of Yugoslavia. President Clinton decided that the United States would be prepared to engage in bombardment of Serbian artillery positions being used to attack Bosnian towns and villages, and he also decided that the United States would be prepared to engage in sanctions against Serbia itself. But he and his senior officials remarked consistently that they would not send ground forces to former Yugoslavia. The United States was prepared to engage in limited operations in Eastern Europe but not to make the kinds of commitments that it had made in Western Europe.

Even if they will not commit themselves to Eastern Europe, however, the American government and most Americans remain committed to defend Western

Europe if it should prove necessary. They also want to keep close ties with America's major European allies—and especially with Germany—even after the cold war. The cutback in America's involvement in global foreign affairs does not mean a loss of interest in Western Europe or in Germany. Instead, it means a redefinition of America's level of involvement and level of expenditure, as well as a desire to share obligations and especially costs.

The American government wants to have friends and allies to help maintain the global concert and to help share in the protection of American and other Western interests. President Bush in May, 1989, reflected these attitudes when he asked West Germany to join the United States as "partners in leadership" even before Germany was united. He did not extend a similar invitation to any other allied nation. Chancellor Helmut Kohl accepted the invitation when he came to Washington in May, 1991. That was the kind of controlled and cooperative redefinition of U.S. global policy that Bush plainly preferred, even if it left room for many interpretations about American (or German) commitments in Europe and the world and even if it ultimately came to be an empty phrase.

Although the U.S. government wishes to divide responsibilities and costs more with others, it is not as ready to divide authority. Washington still believes that it is the leader of a world coalition. It may expect others to listen less attentively than before, but it still expects them to listen. This remains, for America's allies, one of the most difficult aspects of present relationships, and it even remains a problem for America itself. The American domestic discussion of foreign affairs is still dominated by speeches about what America's allies should do, even when the United States itself may be prepared to do very little. Certainly, in matters like Yugoslavia, the U.S. government and the American public will expect major European actions before American forces are committed on a large or definitive scale.

An important reason that America's principal concerns after the end of the cold war are domestic is the genuine revolution that is now going on in the United States.

The United States is now proceeding through a prolonged period of political, economic, and social change. It is simultaneously undergoing geographic, demographic, economic and strategic revolutions. Any one of them would be enough to change the politics and the policies of the country. The combination is doing it faster and more fundamentally.

The part of the United States that is turned toward Europe, and that Europe sees, hears, and regards as representative, is losing in virtually every one of those revolutions. It is resisting them, which is one reason one does not hear very much about them in Europe and one reason many Europeans cannot understand why American decisions are made as they are.

President Ronald Reagan reflected and embodied several of the new revolutions, much more than his successor President Bush and probably more than President Clinton. He was from the Western states and did not believe in big government from Washington. He also believed that the persistent transformation of society is an element of American strength. Compared to Reagan, Bush was essentially a transition figure. It remains unclear whether Clinton will try to reverse those revolutions or to guide them in directions that he himself favors. In either case, he must concentrate enormous political energy on them.

The geographic revolution is most obvious. The population of the country is moving west and southwest, as is the most modern part of American industry. The new life, and the expanding life, has been in California, the Sun Belt, Utah, Nevada, and Washington State. Much of that area has a high Hispanic population and is turned in its thinking very much to Mexico and to Asia. The great cities of the East and Northeast remain prosperous because of their suburbs and because they provide certain services, but virtually every one of them has a hollow core of poverty. They will require immense infusions of resources to be revived.

The demographic revolution is as important as the economic. The country is becoming more heterogeneous. The white population is being replaced by the nonwhite, whether Hispanic, black, or Asian. These groups fuel and support some of the new industries and the new politics. They do not see a Eurocentric world despite the continuing American official interest in Europe.

A massive industrial revolution is taking place at the same time as the other revolutions. Old industries are either dying or being dramatically restructured. The industrial upsurge is in new technologies (in microprocessors, expanded computer memory capacity, telecommunications equipment) and in new production processes (resulting in new hyperplastics and resins that are stronger than steel). The demand for these is not yet enough to maintain a whole economy and may never be, so they cannot fully replace the older industries. But the economic victory in the new industrial revolution will go to those who can combine the old and the new, add a labor force, and capture global markets.

As these processes are continuing, they are fueling closely related debates about economic philosophy, about the future role of the United States in the world, and about the function and cost of government in each. Each debate affects on the others and is in turn influenced by the others, and each can affect American foreign policy.

In economics, the American devotion to Keynesianism and to the welfare state, shaped in the 1930s and 1960s, waned during the recession of 1979–1982, but the precise level of central government intervention in economic management remains very controversial. Such intervention is, of course, regarded as attractive in Washington. New ideas, however, linked to monetarism or to supply-side economics, have entered the arena. They reinforce widespread non-Washington sentiment that less government is better and are part of the reason that the 1992 election became so important and so hard-fought. The American electorate must begin to decide about the role of government in domestic affairs while the importance of government as the maker of foreign policy may be declining.

The doctrinal confusion about economic policy deepened an American economic downturn that would have come without it. It also led to sharp if sometimes submerged debates about industrial policy, monetary policy, trade policy, and the proper U.S. place in the global division of labor. The economic downturn also exacerbated problems that had existed for some time but that had been hidden under the strong economy of the 1980s. Some of those problems, such as migration, deindustrialization, the rise of a high-cost service sector, and the collapse of many urban cores, have further drained resources and have led the United States to focus on itself.

The Western victory in the cold war has given the debates about economic policy and about the role of government a new shape and a new urgency. It has added the future of U.S. foreign policy to the debate. It has brought forth a new concept of a "peace dividend," under which the resources that were spent on foreign policy and defense can be used to solve domestic problems. The phrase implies that all or most of the national budget that has been committed to defense can be used for domestic programs, which is not correct, and there has been a political temptation to spend the "peace dividend" several times over for different purposes.

The "peace dividend" will not, however, be as significant as had been hoped. The defense budget does not allow for as much reduction as many believed during the 1992 campaign and may still believe. Much of it is dedicated to salaries and pensions that cannot be quickly cut. Moreover, the defense budget has a social domestic effect of its own, especially in states and areas where defense industry has long been an important component of the local economy (largely but not exclusively in the West and Southwest). Cutting the defense budget has meant, and may continue to mean, cutting many good jobs in many politically important states. California has suffered massively from those cuts, enough to compensate for the boom in new industries.

The reduction of the defense budget will nonetheless be accelerated after 1992 and 1993 unless there is a global crisis. From fiscal year 1994, it will be possible for the U.S. Congress to transfer funds from the defense budget to the social and domestic budget. Under the budget agreement made between the Congress and Bush in 1990, that has not been possible in the 1992 and 1993 budget years. Therefore, the incentive to cut the defense budget will become all the greater in future years, but it still needs to be done without cutting into too many American jobs.

The foreign portion of the defense budget will, therefore, be cut far more severely than the domestic portion. Money spent in the United States has a positive economic, social and political effect in the state or the community where it is spent. Money spent abroad is essentially spent among foreign voters. Members of the U.S. Congress will be more interested in spending defense money at home, and their effort to secure a "peace dividend" will put heavy pressure on U.S. force deployments abroad. It could have an especially severe effect on deployment in

Germany because of the widespread belief that Germany has adequate resources for its own defense, that it can "pay its own way," and that it is no longer threatened. These kinds of views can become especially important if U.S. actions in Somalia and perhaps in the Balkans become so costly that they impede the widely anticipated reduction in defense costs.

Strategic questions reinforce the financial argument against high expenditures on U.S. forces in Europe. Without the fear of a Soviet attack, what is the purpose of a large expeditionary force? Is it to maintain alliance unity and to continue to provide a German-American link? Is it to provide for the contingency of a Russian return to Bonapartism? Is it to offer U.S. forces for the Middle East a closer place from which to intervene than from the continental United States? For the moment, there is no clear understanding on this in the United States. All the motives may be mixed into one single purpose, but it is hard now to discern that purpose or to see how all the motives will reinforce each other rather than cancel each other out.

Americans cannot, however, decide these issues as easily as before. Isolationism may have been an option one hundred years ago, or perhaps seventy-five or forty-five years ago. But it is not a realistic option now.

Even if there is no overriding anti-Communist basis for foreign and defense policy, there are many U.S. interests around the world. The United States now depends on foreign resources and foreign markets. It cannot exercise its influence unilaterally. It cannot solve domestic problems, because they are too intimately linked with foreign problems, especially in economic matters.

The United States now needs allies and friends even when it does not have enemies. This is the reality that the American government and many American people accept, but they are not yet certain how to meet it.

The American government and the American political system have not yet produced an answer about the future of American foreign policy. Nor will they provide it for some time. The speeches made to date offer only the first reaction, influenced as much by established attitudes as by any realistic projection. The questions that have been raised by the end of the cold war and by the revolutions going on in the United States cannot be answered for several years. Final policies will probably not be decided until the middle of the 1990s. A new consensus may emerge, but its direction remains in doubt.

For just as Germany has its tasks in foreign policy, so does the United States. And the main task is to decide the shape of the world and the role of the United States in that world. As in the years after World War II, it is truly a time for "creation." And, as in the years after World War II, the construction of a new foreign policy and strategy may require many years of planning, debate, and diplomacy as well as force.

The 1992 election did not settle the debate. It produced a government that has a massive domestic agenda but that is also facing a number of immediate crises abroad. Although those crises are not as dangerous as those that confronted the nation during the cold war, they still demand attention and they consume political and strategic assets. There could, therefore, be more serious political and philosophical crises ahead.

Here the role of President Clinton can become crucial. He clearly believes in a stronger government role in the economy and in the commitment of greater resources to America's domestic needs. But he has also made clear that he does not want to spend without restraint. The balance that he can find will have a major effect not only on his own political success but also in the future foreign policy that he and others can conduct. As in Germany, such a balance leaves open many questions about foreign as well as domestic policy.

Of course, the future foreign policy of the United States may well not need the resources that have had to be dedicated to defense and foreign affairs since 1945. The United States will not need as large an army. It will not need to provide military aid to groups that are fighting against insurgencies directed or exploited by the Soviet Union. It can dedicate more resources to other objectives than to foreign affairs.

One of the crucial questions of the 1990s, for Germany and others, will be whether the U.S. government can now find the proper balance between domestic and foreign commitments as well as between total involvement in world affairs and no involvement whatsoever, and whether the United States can formulate effective policies to deal with its allies during that search for a proper balance.

For if Americans decide that they should return to their own historical tradition of a maritime strategy, they might be prepared to envisage less international involvement on distant continents and to withdraw from Europe or to keep only a minimal presence. In that process, they would see Germany very differently from the way they have seen it for the past fifty years.

The American debate, like the German debate, could thus become one of the determining elements of the German-American relationship of the 1990s.

7

THE SEARCH
FOR NEW IDENTITIES

When the Wall came down and Germany was united, Germany acquired a new identity, an identity that went beyond the new borders. At the same time, America also acquired a new identity, even if derivatively.

They must ask themselves if out of these new identities, and out of the new world and the new Europe, must grow a new German-American relationship, and what kind of relationship it can be.

The identity of a new and united Germany is far more difficult to manage than that of West Germany. For it is the old Germany, but it cannot be the old Germany. It must be a Germany that takes responsibility but does not overpower others. It must be a Germany that leads Europe but fits into it. And it must be a Germany that can be a world power without appearing to be one.

That combination may be impossible to effect. There must be moments when the new Germany will act in accordance with its interests as every other state has done throughout history, even if others do not like it. There must be moments when the new Germany will not do what others have grown to expect from West Germany.

For many Germans, the collapse of the Wall was a defining moment. It established the legitimacy of the German nation as a revolutionary people, one that had overcome adversity and had achieved its own freedom in peace. One cannot expect Germans to forget that, even if others do.

For the United States, its new identity will also present an impossible combination. For Americans believe that they have protected and nurtured the freedom of Germany and half the world for almost half a century, and they believe that others should be grateful for what America has done. But the United States has now become a nation more like others, perhaps the only remaining superpower but actually less powerful relative to its allies than it used to be.

Under its new identity, the United States still has the power to lead the world, but it no longer can count on others to follow because of their security needs. Americans cannot expect to have the leading, defining role in every enterprise—especially in Europe. Yet the American government normally expects to command or at least to guide the enterprises in which it is engaged, and it is accustomed to having others either want American leadership or accept it.

The way that Germany and the United States see each other becomes more complicated as well. For Americans will normally expect Germany to understand U.S. policy and will even prefer that Germany support it. German equality and independence are perhaps more difficult for the United States to accept than that of any other country—including even Japan.

The future of German-American relations thus poses many questions:

- Will the United States be prepared to accept a German government that shares its basic interests but pursues many different policies?
- Will Germany be prepared to accept an American government that still maintains a tone of superiority even if the reality of German dependency is past?
- Can the intimacy of the past remain even if the mutual military and diplomatic dependency no longer exists?
- Even if a united Germany still needs some American presence in Europe, and if most of Germany's European allies still want it, can Germany create the conditions that make such a presence possible? And will the United States want it?

The new American and German identities are not what they were when the German-American link was established in the late 1940s. Germany is less dependent, more self-confident, stronger, richer, and more respected. It has found in the new and wider Europe a place to concentrate its energies. America is more ambivalent, less ready to make new commitments, more anxious to remain at home and yet, perhaps paradoxically, still global in its interests and concerns.

United Germany and the United States have been trying to work together in their new relationship since the end of 1990. We will now evaluate that experience against the question posed in the subtitle of this book.

Part Two
GERMAN-AMERICAN RELATIONS SINCE UNIFICATION

8

POLITICAL COOPERATION

Both Germany and the United States want political security for themselves and their friends. They want a stable world in which free nations and free people can feel safe from war, threat, or upheaval. They wanted it during the Cold War, they still want it now, and they will continue to want it.

After German unification, Washington and Bonn wanted to work together to build that kind of security. That was the point of former president Bush's invitation for "partnership in leadership," and many Americans thought that it was the point of Chancellor Kohl's acceptance. Former U.S. secretary of state James Baker and former German foreign minister Hans-Dietrich Genscher expanded the scope of that cooperation further in October, 1991, when they spoke of a "Euro-Atlantic community" that would stretch from Vancouver to Vladivostok. It was to have a North Atlantic Cooperation Council that would bring the transatlantic connection all the way across Siberia, at least in a political, although not in a military, sense.

Political cooperation has, however, not worked smoothly since 1990. The two countries clearly defined "partnership in leadership" differently, and they also expected it to apply in different areas. Although Germany and the United States want common security, they function in different areas, at different levels, and in different ways. They also look at the world from very different locations and historical perspectives. This does not prevent cooperation, and they have cooperated successfully in some parts of the world. But the record since 1990 shows that political cooperation will not always proceed as well as in the past.

THE GERMAN PRIORITY IN EUROPE

Germany functioned primarily in Europe during the cold war and it still continues to do so. Most of its important and immediate political relationships are in Europe, as are its major interests and its greatest areas of concern. The collapse of East Germany and the opening of Eastern Europe have only intensified this European concentration by opening new perspectives in Europe itself and also by posing new problems in Europe.

The German government, as well as German business executives and intellectuals, do not see Eastern Europe or even the states of the former Soviet Union as distant and alien entities. Many Germans regard Prague, Budapest, Warsaw, Kiev and St. Petersburg as European cities. Just as many Germans were never prepared to accept the division of Germany as much as many foreigners were, they also regarded the division of Europe as artificial. They want to reestablish former ties to the states of Central and Eastern Europe, effectively putting Germany back into the center of the continent. Businesspeople see new openings for trade and investment. Intellectuals see the chance to begin new and fascinating dialogues.

Before the opening to the East, Germany had taken upon itself the basic responsibility of shaping a stronger Western Europe and European Community, and this objective has not changed. Kohl and Genscher, like their predecessors, spearheaded every effort to strengthen the EC politically as well as economically, and the current foreign minister, Klaus Kinkel, will undoubtedly do the same. Before and at the Maastricht summit of heads of state and heads of government of the European Community in December, 1991, both Kohl and Genscher called for a stronger and more democratic European entity.

The German government has also tried assiduously to make certain that any major German foreign policy moves will be coordinated or at least discussed with other EC states, even when there is disagreement within the Community itself. The EC states do not want Germany to be isolated in Europe, as it was before. Germany has supported every effort to expand the operations and the responsibilities of the Community.

In doing so, Germany has helped to alter the character of the Community itself. From its beginnings as a customs union and an economic area, the EC has increasingly become an organ for political consultation and coordination. Like the G-7, although somewhat more formally, it provides a forum for discussion of many urgent political issues. As the G-7 has become the governing board of the global concert, so the EC Council has become the governing board of a potentially evolving new concert of Europe.

Even as Germany has advanced the integration of Western Europe, it has long been working for closer ties with the former Soviet Union and Eastern Europe. *Ostpolitik,* initiated by the West German grand coalition under Chancellor Georg Kiesinger and expanded powerfully under Chancellor Willy Brandt, became a firm constant of German foreign policy before 1990. That policy created broad economic and cultural links between West Germany on the one hand and the Soviet Union and most East European states on the other.

The opening of the Wall has reinforced the German determination to continue to build a strong European Community and also to take the Community with Germany to the East. Germany has used the Community since 1990 as a new organ of *Ostpolitik* that would not jeopardize Bonn's ties to the West as Germany advances into the East. Chancellor Kohl told a meeting of the Bertelsmann Forum on April 3, 1992, that Germany had to deepen the EC in the West while also using it to overcome the division of Europe between East and West.

Even beyond the Community, Germany has worked consistently since 1990 to broaden East-West links in Europe and to strengthen the new lines that run across the continent. Kohl took the initiative in organizing aid for the Commonwealth of Independent States (CIS), the former Soviet Union, and for the separate states within the CIS. Under his leadership, Germany has signed treaties establishing new relations with Central European states despite continuing land and property claims by some Germans and despite lingering East European suspicions and even fears of Germany.

Germany has also given more aid than any other country to Russia, Central Europe, and Eastern Europe. On May 5, 1992, Kohl told the Association of American Newspaper Publishers that Germany had already provided DM 75 billion for the CIS and DM 105 billion for all Central, Eastern and Southeastern European countries, and he added that Germany had reached the limits of its capacity. Germany has also made clear that its aid was to be used not only in Russia itself but in the newly independent republics. German aid and investment represented far more than half of all the aid and investment coming to the CIS from the West.

The Germans have not hesitated to call on the U.S. and other Western governments to help. During a G-7 meeting in January, 1992, and at the Munich G-7 summit in July, 1992, Kohl and other Germans pressed hard for "burden-sharing" in aid. The chancellor specifically told President Bush at Camp David that he hoped for a large American commitment because the American interest in European stability would logically appear to be as great as the German. The chancellor helped personally to shape the program for international aid to the CIS that President Bush announced in March, 1992, and he supported Russian president Boris Yeltsin's plea for more assistance in Munich. Germany has also tried to help arrange a larger Japanese contribution to the CIS, and Genscher once offered to mediate the Russo-Japanese dispute regarding the Kurile Islands in order to help promote Japanese aid to Russia.

Germany has taken other steps to help the CIS and Eastern Europe. With the support of other West European countries and over lingering U.S. opposition, German diplomats and trade officials pushed hard to ease restrictions on technology exports to the former Communist states. They were successful in promoting the May, 1992, agreement loosening those restrictions, especially because senior Americans also began to believe that the restrictions made little commercial sense and could jeopardize democratic development in former Communist states. Germany pressed for Russian membership in the International Monetary Fund (IMF) and pledged its share for a fund to stabilize the ruble.

However, at the Munich summit Kohl did not support Bush's suggestion that Russia be invited to join the G-7, for the G-7 summit membership not only included an economic role but—more important—an implied political role for Russia in the world as a whole. Unlike the United States, Germany was not prepared to share its membership in the global concert.

German embassies and trade missions have opened in all the new states, well before those of other Western governments. Senior German politicians have visited virtually every CIS state and East European state. Genscher was the most widely traveled Western foreign minister in the CIS until Secretary Baker took a tour of those states in February, 1992. By the same token, the senior officials of all those states have come to Germany more often than to any other Western state including the United States.

Germany has quickly established the greatest economic influence of any Western state in Eastern Europe and the CIS, sometimes to the discomfort of East European political and economic leaders who would welcome a more balanced Western presence. German production norms are being adopted throughout the area, as are German financial and banking principles. German bankers and businessmen are everywhere, helping to provide funds and also making their own investments. Daimler-Benz, Volkswagen, Siemens and other giant German firms have set out investment programs involving billions of D-marks, often edging out their Western competitors in an area that German executives describe as the new growth opportunity in Europe. German official commitments dwarf those of other Westerners, including the United States, although American private investment is ahead of Germany's. In all the new states, the Deutsche mark is either the second or third (behind the dollar) currency. It would probably be more widely accepted ahead of the dollar if so many East Europeans were not afraid of European political crises.

All these measures are intended to promote political stability as well as a German presence. The German government wants to maximize its economic aid in order to maximize the prospects for stability in the East. German government officials insist that democracy cannot be permitted to fail as Communism did, and they will do what they can to make it succeed.

German officials are not oblivious to events outside Europe, but those events have a much lower priority. Genscher visited Japan in February 1992, but it was his first visit in six years, and he used his visit largely to urge greater Japanese support for German aid to Russia. The Germans remain principally concentrated on Europe, where they have the greatest influence, the greatest commitment, and the greatest reason to fear if things go wrong. German officials, who have long had to concentrate on preserving Germany's safety and prosperity in Europe, do not yet have the wider global vision that the Japanese, Americans, or the officials of other maritime states acquired over time.

THE AMERICAN GLOBAL VIEW

Unlike Germany, the United States ranges across the width of a continent. It opens on two oceans and several other seas. Above, it explores open space. It is a true world power. It has always believed that it could choose its own priorities and the areas in which it wanted to intervene. It has worldwide bases and air and naval forces as well as an enormous arsenal of nuclear weapons. The latter may now appear less important, as the opponent they were mainly intended to deter no longer exists, but they form the reserve which warns all nations that America wishes to remain unchallenged.

More important than American power for its own sake is the role of the United States as the leader of the global concert. It is in this role that Americans often see themselves, if unconsciously. They may call it being "leader of the free world" or the "sole remaining superpower," but it is part of the U.S. sense of engagement in the world and leadership of the world. It also reflects an American sense of responsibility for what may happen anywhere. It is part of the American global presence.

The United States perceives its interests as being almost everywhere. It has allies and close friends not only in Europe but in Asia, the Middle East, and the Americas. While no American likes to be called a "policeman of the world," Americans do not hesitate to use their power if U.S. interests are directly or indirectly threatened. Only a U.S. president would make an inaugural address that pledges intervention anywhere at any time under certain circumstances. American air, naval, or ground forces have been deployed or committed to combat on every continent since World War II. Few years have gone by without U.S. forces being involved in one or another operation somewhere. Some American political leaders may criticize selected U.S. military engagements, but most approve such engagements when they see the interests of the nation or of their constituents threatened. They do not challenge the notion that America has a global role, even if they complain about the costs.

Some broad principles have guided the size and type of U.S. international engagements. U.S. forces have usually been committed when it appeared that the balance of power in one or another continent might shift to America's disadvantage and when an American role might help to maintain the balance. They have also been more committed in areas that the American government regarded as geopolitically vital. American commitments have followed a logical if perhaps unconscious and unarticulated pattern, and those who have argued against those commitments have usually argued that they violated the agreed pattern.

American attitudes have changed with the passing of the cold war, even if U.S. interests have not. Americans want to use their own resources more for domestic purposes. They are also acutely conscious that those resources are limited, and they want others to help them more than before. As in the past, the United States continues to regard itself as the leader of a global concert and of a global alliance system. It also keeps a wary eye out for threats in the areas where it has particular interests. But it now wants its allies to do more to help sustain the global system and worldwide security. What has changed is not the American readiness to act, which remains in place, but the American readiness to act alone. Now, the U.S. government and the U.S. public want others to join and also to help pay the cost.

In particular, the U.S. government and the American public believe that the wealthy friends whom the Americans have protected from nuclear threats for many years should now contribute more to the common effort. As the Americans see it, only they could respond to the nuclear threat because Germany and Japan could not. But the new threats can be met by Germany—or Europe—and Japan as well as by the United States, and those states should do more to help support the global system.

Many American military even believe that this is part of the function that American power serves for its friends. They fear that an American refusal to act in certain circumstances, especially if Germany or Japanese interests are threatened by a nuclear power, might stimulate Germany and Japan to ask for their own nuclear weapons. Thus, the American global commitment helps to forestall potentially damaging debate in the domestic politics of America's friends.

The American government and the American body politic have long assumed, and still assume, that Germans share the American view of world events even if Germany could not intervene as the United States did. Now that Germany is united, they believe that at least some of the German inhibitions should fall. Even if Germany does not obtain nuclear weapons, Germany should help more in bearing the global burdens carried by the United States. The American government also believes that Germany can now share the cost of managing a global policy better than in the past because it no longer has to help maintain the East-West border in Europe. The major U.S. role in having promoted German unification despite the reservations of other states reinforces the American belief that Germany will help.

The U.S. government has always expected German agreement with U.S. views and even a certain deference to American sensibilities. This has changed slightly with German unification, for many Americans understand that German interests may not coincide with American interests as much as in the past. The U.S. government does not expect Germany to be as dependent as before. Nor does it expect Germany to agree with all American policies and propositions or to support the United States merely out of a sense of obligation. But it does believe that Germany will and should be its most loyal and most steadfast continental European ally and the one whose interests will most frequently coincide with those of the United States. It also believes that Germany should continue to help sustain the presence of the global concert in Europe, for Germany is a member of the global concert and should want to keep the concert as powerful as possible.

For the United States, Europe is only a small if important part of the world, even if it may be the part that Germany regards as the main arena for its own interests. The U.S. government may perceive some of the same problems that Germany sees to its east, such as the potentially dangerous implications of chaos, coups, or ethnic conflict in Russia, between the CIS states, or in Eastern Europe. But the end of the cold war means that the global power balance does not turn on Europe as it did. Moreover, many Americans have paradoxically taken their eyes off Europe as a potential crisis spot at the very moment when European stability may be coming under greater threat. Only a sharp reminder from former president Richard Nixon in March 1992 alerted the White House fully to the dangers that a Russian return to dictatorship might bring, and the U.S. Congress will not in the foreseeable future or under foreseeable circumstances be prepared to help Russia as much as Germany will be prepared to help. When the Soviet Union as a global power was supplanted by Russia as a large European power, American interest in its problems and prospects was bound to decline, although American relations with Russia can be expected to improve over time.

President Bush did begin to pay more attention in the spring of 1992 to the aid needs of Russia and other CIS states, but he faced opposition in the U.S. Congress. His first request for almost half a billion dollars was long ignored, and he was denounced for wanting to spend money in Russia when Americans needed it at home. Although U.S. grain sales to the CIS states found financing, other types of aid were delayed. Russian president Boris Yeltsin's visit to Washington in June, 1992, created some sense of urgency and helped produce greater Democratic congressional support for aid to Russia, but the American level of assistance to Russia and the CIS will never reach the same levels as Germany's. The United States joined the IMF financing effort after Germany, also largely because there were many questions in the Congress.

Even after the meeting between President Bill Clinton and Chancellor Helmut Kohl in April, 1993, in which Kohl pressed hard for additional U.S. aid to Russia, Clinton only pledged $1.8 billion, a pittance compared to almost $55 billion in German aid. Even that comparatively modest amount of American aid was expected to run into stiff opposition in the U.S. Congress.

However, the United States can help Germany and Western Europe in other ways, especially in the nuclear arena and in permitting Russia and other CIS states to turn former Soviet military resources to civilian purposes. The agreements reached by Presidents Bush and Yeltsin to reduce nuclear strategic weapons, like the agreements negotiated between Secretary Baker and the foreign ministers of Belarus, Ukraine, and Kazakhstan, not only helped contribute to European stability but also helped Russian and other CIS leaders to concentrate more resources on the civilian economy.

In their broad approach to the former Soviet Union, therefore, Germany and the United States have generally cooperated even if they have followed different timetables and if they have concentrated on different aspects of the problem. It has proven to be a case of successful complementarity, where both states did different things but served a similar objective.

If there is an American concern about Europe, however, it is no longer about Russia or about Eastern Europe. It is mainly about the direction that Western Europe will take. The American government wants to keep the major states of Western Europe in the global concert and it wants West European support for global objectives that it regards as universal. It wants a Europe that shares the U.S. view of the world and that is prepared to work with the United States to maintain the global structures and institutions that the United States created and that the

West Europeans have joined. It believes that those structures have served the common interest. It even needs to have Europe remain in the global concert, for no concert can be successful if Europe is not a part of it. And the United States fears a separate West European path in political, military, and economic affairs.

The purpose of the global concert, as defined by the United States and by other members, has essentially been to establish and to maintain a global system that suits the needs and interests of the members and of other states associated with them. It has also been intended to promote global peace, stability, and prosperity. For a long time, this was primarily defined as a common struggle against the Soviet Union and the Communist system. But it could and did go further. It could mean promoting democracy and human rights; it could mean an international structure that would encourage third world development or orderly migration and aid to refugees; it could mean maintaining access to raw materials, to markets, and to bases; or it could mean an open and smoothly functioning global commercial and monetary system. After 1990, the anti-Communist objective has become virtually irrelevant, but the global system envisaged by the United States has other interests than anti-Communism.

In the context of that global system, the United States has been much more ready than many other states to give Germany a leading role. The American government has supported German permanent membership in the U.N. Security Council, although France and Great Britain have opposed it. The United States has been ready to promote greater German involvement internationally. It has done so under the assumption that such involvement would support U.S. as well as German interests, but it has often found that Bonn and the German body politic were less ready to act than Washington wished.

DISSONANCE AND COOPERATION
IN THE GULF

Despite their common purposes in the European phase of the cold war, united Germany and the United States have not yet devised a common purpose in dealing with problems that might face the global concert outside Europe. They have disagreed as to what might or might not constitute a challenge. Washington would see universal challenges that Bonn might see as special American problems.

Such differences go back to the time when Germany was divided. But they became more severe after 1990 because the American government now expects a united German government to be more helpful to American global policies, while Germany wants to concentrate on Europe. But the work of global political cooperation, including the selective use of military force, has not waited for Bonn and Washington to sort out their differences.

Even before German unification, West Germany and the United States were to have sharp arguments about German business activities around the world and particularly in the Middle East. The single most emotional incident occurred in

1988–1989, when evidence began accumulating about German sales of machinery that could be used to manufacture poison gas at an alleged pharmaceutical plant at Rabta in Libya. When Chancellor Kohl did not react quickly to President Ronald Reagan's request that those sales be investigated and stopped, the American press began a series of revelations. Those included an article entitled "Auschwitz-in-the-Sand," which alleged that German companies were helping to manufacture gas to be used against Jews in Israel as it had been used against Jews in concentration camps.

After bitterly emotional exchanges between German and U.S. officials, including a remark by Volker Rühe, now Germany's defense minister, that Americans were skating on thin ice in this matter and that "the ice is thinner than many think," enough evidence accumulated to show that at least one German company was indeed shipping questionable machinery to Libya. The German government stopped the sales and prosecuted the company. The German government also introduced legislation to block such sales in future, which satisfied the U.S. government but not members of the U.S. Congress, who continued to criticize Germany.

After German unification, the most pronounced differences between Bonn and Washington arose with respect to the Gulf War of 1991 and to the crisis in Yugoslavia in 1991 and 1992.

The Gulf crisis that followed the Iraqi invasion of Kuwait showed that a united Germany was not inclined to undertake global obligations and that it might even hesitate about some European obligations. The German government did not send combat forces to the Gulf despite U.S. requests for at least some support, although it did send minesweepers to the Eastern Mediterranean. There were persistent reports that the Germans hesitated because of a Soviet warning that the deployment of German forces to the Gulf would jeopardize Supreme Soviet ratification of German unity and might delay the departure of Soviet troops from Germany.

But more fundamental attitudes were also at work. Although U.S. officials pointed out that they had not asked Germany to participate in the forces assembled under General Norman Schwarzkopf's command in the Gulf, there were bruised feelings in Washington about the slowness of the German reaction to the crisis and about the evident German wish to remain uninvolved in a situation that the U.S. government believed should concern others as much as itself.

Many American officials were disturbed by German hints that Bonn might not honor its NATO commitment to Turkey if Iraq attacked Turkey because of air operations conducted from Turkish bases. Germany delayed its contribution to the Ace Mobile Force in Turkey by several weeks, despite a specific Turkish request in the NATO Defense Planning Committee. German officials wondered out loud whether Turkey was trying to use the Kuwait crisis for its own possible aggrandizement or to advance the political ambitions of senior Turkish politicians. But many Turks and many Americans complained that the Germans, who had been defended for decades by other NATO forces, now were less ready to help others when the threat was not on Germany's borders. The American and British governments were particularly critical, but even the French and Italian governments joined in. The Italians pointed out that their own forces had been dispatched to Turkey more quickly than had the German forces.

Germany did help the American and U.N. effort indirectly, and especially through logistic support. It arranged priority handling for U.S. and other forces going to the Gulf, especially for the U.S. VII Corps. About two-thirds of U.S. land and air forces in the Gulf operation came from Europe, many from Germany, and they would not have been able to get to the Gulf as quickly if Germany had not helped to send them. With its logistic support, Germany made a major contribution to the war effort, although it chose to keep the contribution quiet. Germany also helped finance the allied war effort by helping the United States with its costs, and the German contribution was fully paid before that of any other state.

During the early phases of the Gulf crisis, two rather different parts of the same debate went on in Bonn and Washington and exacerbated each other. In Bonn, the debate pitted Germany's loyalties to its main ally against the Federal Republic's long-standing and highly popular determination to avoid involving Germany's forces outside NATO. In Washington, the debate aroused the usual complaints that America's allies were not carrying their share of the global burden. Many members of Congress accused Germany and Japan of ignoring all that Americans had done to rebuild and defend them after World War II and of wanting to enrich themselves under the American umbrella while running away when the chips were down.

The German government finally ended the German part of the debate by asserting that Germany's constitution prohibited sending German forces outside the NATO area. This constitutional interpretation, which some American as well as German lawyers questioned, was an attempt to solve a political debate by legal means. But it gave the German government a reason to do what it and most Germans wanted.

The debate also revealed ambivalent attitudes about Germany that still existed in the United States. While some Americans argued that Germany had now outgrown the Hitler legacy and could participate in global operations like any other country, others still invoked that legacy and used a tone of moral superiority in arguing either for or against German involvement. The tone as much as the substance of the American debate left many Germans both confused and angry, and they especially resented being accused of neglecting their loyalty to the United States by failing to send military forces after Americans had long told Germans that they should abandon their militarist tradition.

The old issue about German equipment sales for military purposes also arose again. The fact that a number of German companies had sold equipment that could perhaps produce poison gas made the accusations against Germany even harsher. Later revelations indicated that German exporters had also supplied Iraq with centrifuges that could have been used by the Iraqi government for uranium enrichment and that could have helped Iraq develop and produce atomic bombs. They also suggested that Germany had sold potential rocket parts and equipment to Iraq. There would have been a major crisis in German-American relations if any Iraqi Scud missile had hit Israel with a chemical warhead that might have been manufactured with German machinery.

The German government again had to deal with its exporters and export regulations. The government arrested a number of German executives who had sold potential rocket components and other equipment that Iraq could have used for military purposes. Following the regulations that it had introduced after the Rabta revelations—and that had obviously proven inadequate—the government in April 1992 introduced new regulations further tightening export controls on material that could be diverted for military purposes. But it also warned that Germany alone could not prevent the global availability of dual-use equipment that could have military utility.

The United States itself began to face growing embarrassment as more information about foreign military assistance to Iraq surfaced in late 1991 and in 1992. It became evident that the Germans had not been alone in helping Iraq, but that many countries—including the United States—had helped finance and build the Iraqi war machine directly and indirectly. American documents indicated that Iraq had been able to acquire potential dual-use equipment in the United States as well as elsewhere. The documents showed that the American government, hoping to use Iraq to balance the fundamentalist Muslim regime in Iran, had substantially built up the regime of Iraqi dictator Saddam Hussein. They also suggested that U.S. food aid to Iraq had been diverted for Iraqi arms purchases with U.S. knowledge, and that officials in the U.S. Department of Energy might have suppressed internal reports warning that Iraq was building an atomic bomb.

Although the U.S. government denied these allegations, further investigations are certain to follow and may reveal even more information about American equipment finding its way to Iraq or about U.S. aid being misused by Iraq. Whatever may emerge, it would help blunt American criticism of German sales, although it would not solve the problem for either country.

The Iraqi crisis also precipitated a sharp debate in Germany itself about the purposes for which German forces could be sent outside the NATO area to which they had restricted themselves for the past four decades. The German political parties took different positions, and it was clear that it would take many years before a full consensus emerged. By mid-1992, however, there was broad agreement that German forces could participate in humanitarian operations under the U.N. flag, so-called blue helmet operations, and a small group of German soldiers were sent on such a mission to Cambodia. Further potential missions, such as peace-keeping or peace-making, remained in dispute, with the government parties being more prepared to consider such missions than were the opposition parties.

THE YUGOSLAV CRISIS

The dissolution of Yugoslavia during 1991 and 1992 raised a different set of complexities for Bonn and Washington, for it happened in Europe and not in the Middle East. It showed that the German and American governments would react differently to a European and a non-European matter. It also raised questions about the extent to which the United States, as an essentially maritime power, would be prepared to engage in Eastern and Southeastern Europe. Like the Gulf war, however, it led to some nasty backbiting between U.S. and German officials.

If there was ever a situation made for German-American disagreement, it was the ethnic crisis that reached a boiling point in Yugoslavia in 1991 after having simmered off and on ever since the formation of the Yugoslav Kingdom in the aftermath of World War I.

Yugoslavia had been created in the victors' treaties after the First World War, especially the treaties of St. Germain, Neuilly, and Trianon, largely out of territory taken from states that had been Germany's allies in the war. During World War II, Adolf Hitler and Benito Mussolini had split the country, but it was reconstituted after the war under the leadership of Marshal Broz Tito, who had led the resistance against the Axis. During the cold war, relations between Bonn and Belgrade had gone up and down but had generally been good, in part because of a large community of Yugoslav workers in Germany.

The United States had also enjoyed generally good relations with Yugoslavia despite Tito's showy brand of neutralism. Many Americans admired Yugoslavia for its independent role in Eastern Europe under the shadow of the Soviet empire. When the Yugoslav crisis erupted in 1991, both the U.S. national security adviser, General Brent Scowcroft, and the U.S. deputy secretary of state, Lawrence Eagleburger, were old Yugoslav hands who had served in Belgrade (Eagleburger as ambassador) and who had later enjoyed consultant relationships with Yugoslav authorities and Yugoslav companies.

In 1991 an open split developed between Bonn and Washington. The United States supported the unity of Yugoslavia despite intelligence analyses indicating that the country was about to disintegrate. Secretary of State James Baker went out of his way during a visit to Belgrade in June of the year to win pledges from each of the constituent republics to do nothing that would jeopardize Yugoslav unity. He made a speech committing the United States to Yugoslav unity, even at a time when the constituent republics were seething with revolt. But Bonn made clear that it no longer supported Yugoslav unity and that it was prepared to recognize Slovenia and Croatia when they declared independence.

At the end of 1991, against the advice of Secretary Baker and of retiring U.N. secretary general Xavier Pérez de Cuellar, Bonn pressed the European Community to join in recognizing the two states. This was not an easy decision for many Community members, especially France and Britain, which together had helped create Yugoslavia and preferred it to remain an entity. The American government lobbied hard against the EC decision, and there were press reports that some EC members (especially France) supported Germany mainly to show their independence from the United States.

The U.S. government, burned by the experience of having its secretary of state embarrassed and several of its senior officials accused of financially motivated partisanship, thereupon pulled back and chose essentially to let the Europeans—and the Germans—take the lead. It ceased to support Yugoslav integrity and recognized the independence of the separate republics, joining the Europeans in also recognizing Bosnia-Herzegovina, but it generally withdrew from any attempts to solve or guide developments in former Yugoslavia.

By the spring of 1992, however, the breakup of Yugoslavia had led to extraordinary violence, especially in Bosnia-Herzegovina, where the intermingling of populations made ethnically homogenous areas virtually impossible to establish. The "Yugoslav" army led by Serbia, as well as ethnic Serbian militia units, attacked the other populations and shelled the Bosnian capital of Sarajevo. An estimated two million refugees fled. The European Community was paralyzed by disagreements about possible differences between Germany and France over stronger action to be taken against Serbia. Western television showed grisly pictures of civilian casualties in Bosnia, again forcing the United States to engage.

Washington and European governments, including the German, began working together more closely, and the United States took the lead more and more. The United States and the West Europeans agreed to diplomatic sanctions against a common break in relations with the Belgrade government. The United States took the initiative to obtain a U.N. Security Council resolution calling for stiff economic sanctions against Serbia. Sharp American criticism of Serbia led to a Serbian cease-fire offer, which, however, came too late to deter the Security Council. Although the American government continued to insist that it would not send any troops to Yugoslavia, American leadership had clearly helped to bring about international action. But few observers thought the killing would stop.

As Serbian army and militia attacks continued, Bush and the other G-7 leaders agreed in Munich to send more relief to Bosnia and specifically to Sarajevo. Kinkel decided to let German aircraft fly relief missions. He and Defense Minister Volker Rühe, with the chancellor's approval, decided to send German naval vessels to the Adriatic. President Bush also decided to send U.S. naval units to the Adriatic and to let U.S. aircraft fly supporting missions to protect relief flights. But the United States, like Germany, did not want to become engaged militarily, and Bush in particular did not want to have American ground forces engaged in an endless East European struggle during an American election year.

The reengagement of the United States in the Yugoslav crisis showed that forceful U.S. backing remained essential for any U.N. decision, especially because only Washington could persuade the former Soviet Union and China either to support such action or to abstain. It also demonstrated that, despite greater European independence from the United States, American involvement could sometimes be necessary to produce a forceful EC action when the Europeans were divided. Germany could perhaps persuade a reluctant EC Council to take some steps—like diplomatic recognition—but not others. Although the United States continued to make clear, as it had from the time of the Czech coup at the beginning of the Cold War in 1948, that its vital interests were not as much at stake in Eastern Europe as in Western Europe, the American role could still prove helpful and perhaps decisive.

The Yugoslav crisis also starkly revealed the danger that the new Europe would witness the return of nationalism, tribalism, and terrorism, which had plagued the old Europe and had almost destroyed the continent. The crisis echoed the Balkan disputes that had helped to bring on World War I. The tensions between Slovenia and Croatia on the one hand and the Serbian-dominated Yugoslav government on the other brought back images of the confrontations between Serbia and the Austro-Hungarian empire.

The Yugoslav crisis even threw into sharp focus the arguments among the West Europeans themselves, arguments that often left them unable to take joint action. The ugly problem of the Balkans had arisen again, this time to complicate the building of a united Europe. Like all Balkan crises, it was carried by emotions that no outsider could hope to contain or to channel. And, like all Balkan crises, it drew outsiders into situations where they could not prevail and that they could not control. It also raised questions about the European Community's capacity to act in a political crisis.

To the Germans, sitting closest to the edge of Eastern Europe, the Yugoslav crisis was a grim reminder that the new Europe would present genuine threats and that Germany might not be able to rely on the United States as it often had in the past. For although Germany had been able to get American support at several crucial junctures, Washington also made clear that Bonn could not consistently count on that kind of support. Washington officials still smarted at the defeat that they had suffered when the EC supported Germany against U.S. advice.

In the Yugoslav crisis, as in the Gulf War, Germany was suddenly much more exposed than before. The German decision to recognize Slovenia and Croatia brought forth the old arguments about Germany being too "assertive" and even "aggressive." When German diplomats met with others to present their views, American newspapers reported that the Germans were exerting "pressure tactics" and that they were "demanding" that others follow their wishes.

These kinds of words, seldom used to describe the actions of others, irritated many Germans and convinced them that they could do no right. The Germans complained that they were constantly being accused of being either too assertive or too reticent, too demanding or too diffident, and that those who disagreed with German policies kept evoking unpleasant images of Germany's past and re-treating behind old anti-German clichés instead of debating the issues on their merits. Washington and Bonn found that they needed to concentrate a great deal of effort not only on the substance but also on the tone of their discussion.

The prospect for closer coordination between American and German policies and effort improved toward the second half of 1992, when the new foreign minister, Klaus Kinkel, took office. He showed early on that he believed in a somewhat less literal interpretation of the limits on German readiness to act internationally. Thus, when the civil war in Yugoslavia intensified, he led an effort within the German government to participate more actively than in the past. He and the new defense minister, Volker Rühe, ordered a naval vessel to patrol the Adriatic off the shore of Croatia. But even he could not move too far too fast. The German vessel had different rules of engagement from other allied vessels involved in the blockade against Serbia. It was not permitted to inspect suspected vessels, but it did go so far as to point to vessels that might be heading toward ports in the former Yugoslavia. Later, when there was some discussion of a potential military enforcement of the "no-fly" area over parts of the former Yugoslavia, Kinkel objected to having German forces and even German surveillance aircraft take part in that enforcement.

When President Clinton decided to engage in bombing operations against Serbian artillery positions, Germany was able to support the U.S. action politically although it was still unable to commit its own forces. The German government did decide, however, that it would permit some of its reconnaissance aircraft to be used to help enforce an embargo on shipment of goods to Serbia as well as a "no-fly" zone over Bosnia. That was a revolutionary step, which took place only after a review by the German Constitutional Court, and it helped bring the German and American positions closer together. The Germans have made clear, however, that they will not finance American and U.N. operations in Yugoslavia as they had done during the Gulf War.

The limited coordination between American and German actions strengthened the hands of those in Germany who believed that the day would come when Germany would be more free to play an active international role. It also, however, illustrated the different realities under which American and German policy could be conducted.

The German government showed itself more prepared to act, however, when the United States later in 1992 led an international humanitarian effort to protect the relief shipment to the starving victims of the civil war in Somalia. Although the first forces that went into Somalia were American and others, especially French, British, and Italian, the German government announced that it would be prepared to send a contingent of 1,500 soldiers to help with a U.N. relief effort even if it could not participate in military operations. Peace would have to be established before German forces could function.

The German government did attempt to initiate the possibility of wider action. The ruling parties agreed in January 1993 to amend the Basic Law in order that German forces would be permitted to participate in (1) peace-keeping operations under a Security Council resolution or under a regional organization, (2) peace-making operations authorized by the Security Council, and (3) enforcement of the right of collective self-defense under the U.S. Charter with other states, even without a Security Council resolution. In the latter case, the action would have to be approved by a two-thirds majority of the Bundestag, not the simple majority required for the first two. Nonetheless, the opposition Social Democrats made clear that they would not approve amending the German Basic Law in that sense. U.N. Secretary General Boutros Boutros-Ghali told the German government during a visit to Bonn during the same month that Germany needed to resolve this issue if it was to play a full role in the United Nations.

The coincidence of the Gulf, Yugoslavia, and Somalia crises within the immediate aftermath of German unification offered the chance to see both the positive and negative elements of German-American global cooperation in action. The crises showed that certain common interests remained even after the end of the cold war. But they also showed, especially in the American but also in the German debates, some of the tensions that had built up after forty years of close German-American relations and a carefully and deliberately constricted German international role.

The fact that many Germans all too often saw the Gulf crisis as a German-American issue rather than as a test of Germany's new world role, and the frequent American tendency to denounce German policy both in the Gulf and in Yugoslavia, left many bruised feelings on both sides. Even if the new political relationship could work in dealing with Moscow, it would not always work easily and it would certainly not work around the world as a whole.

The crises also showed, however, on due reflection, that Germany was moving toward a more active role in global crises although it would need to take more time before concrete decisions could be made. The German government and opposition split, with the opposition Social Democratic Party insisting that German forces could only serve as peace-keepers in U.N. operations like the one in Cambodia. The government was more prepared to have German forces serve in what were termed "peace-making" operations in which active military engagements might take place, but it was not prepared to send German forces into military conflicts. Even within the government, such parties as the chancellor's CDU (Christian Democratic Union) or its sister party the CSU (Christian Social Union) were more prepared to act than was the foreign minister's FDP (Free Democratic Party).

Most of all, the various crises showed that Germany needed time above everything else in order to understand its own new international role. Unfortunately, that time might not be available, and all too often it was the American government that had to remind the Germans of that reality. Other European governments could and did join American-led efforts in various international operations. But Germany remained constrained.

The crises also showed that Germany's membership in the global concert remained limited in a number of fundamental ways despite Germany's strength, affluence, and power in Europe. Other members of the concert could and would act, and even Japan appeared to have less of a burden to face than Germany did. To the degree to which the U.S. government was prepared to make such common action a test of alliance loyalty, German-American relations would suffer. They would also suffer to the degree to which Germans would decide that it was their American ally rather than the force of circumstances that was forcing these decisions upon a reluctant German political and public consciousness.

The United States was gradually becoming the midwife for a greater German international role, whether in Europe or beyond Europe, and in this process the German internal debate might be distorted into an element of the German-American debate. America was forcing the pace, and Germans were considering their policies not only in light of their own global interests but in light of their readiness to follow America's guidance. This could not, over the long run, serve as a healthy element in German-American links.

The future elements of the debate, however, appear to be clear. The United States will remain more prepared to intervene internationally than Germany will be, but it will continue to ask for German support. Gradually, over time, Germany will probably be prepared to offer ever more support—especially if it can be coordinated through international institutions of one kind or another. One day, Germany will probably be prepared to play a greater international role, and the German people will be prepared to accept such a role—whether in Europe or beyond.

At the end of the debate, German-American cooperation might be stronger than before if the two countries genuinely agree on what to do. It might also, however, be weaker than before if they do not agree or if they have compromised their relations by permitting some distant global problem to become a German-American issue. They will need to adjust their dialogue to strengthen the likelihood of cooperation and to avoid the kind of distorted argument that could hurt their common enterprise.

It is to the advantage of both Germany and the United States that Germany's international role evolve in the context of German interests as perceived by the Germans themselves, and that it is defined within that context rather than in the context of German deference to the United States. For Germany's role will need to grow, largely because the breadth of Germany's interests will need to grow and because Germany cannot count on others to protect that wider range of interests as they used to protect Germany's rather narrow range of interests. And the evolution of that debate will constitute one of the core elements of German-American relations during the coming decade.

In the initial years after German unity, however, neither the German nor the American government found the way toward the kind of dialogue that will be necessary to build a sound foundation for future international political cooperation. Nor have they together yet found a way to coordinate their actions within the context of the global concert that they helped to shape. In the crucial areas where they began by having sharp differences, they both needed a long time and some harsh words before they were finally able to support each other by complementary if not identical policies.

For Washington, the very purpose of the global concert requires close cooperation throughout the world. For Bonn, the concert has functioned in some parts of Europe and not elsewhere. Germans cannot conceive that they might be involved in applying elsewhere the principles that they want to see applied in Europe.

*   *   *

The German joy at having achieved unity is tempered by the sudden awareness that others now expect precisely what the Germans are least able to offer at this particular time. The American joy at cold war victory is tempered by the awareness that they cannot count on their old associates to be as immediately supportive in dealing with new problems as they appeared to be in dealing with the old. The two governments have not defined and understood their remaining common interests, and they have not yet even seriously discussed those topics. Therefore, they have all too often found it impossible to reach common policies. One of the highest priorities of the German-American dialogue over the next several years must be to reach a consensus on this question, and especially to agree on what role Germany can and should play in the world as a whole.

9

ECONOMIC COORDINATION

Now that the cold war is ended, people and governments everywhere will concentrate much more on their economic situation. They regard economic security as their most urgent and vital concern. Nations will live or die, and governments stand or fall, on their ability to take care of their people's economic needs and wishes. Most states in recorded history have not been able to do that, and they have often substituted demagogy for prosperity; but people have now come to expect prosperity or at least to want it.

But no state can count on achieving economic security for its citizens in isolation. No economy can prosper when others decline. The lines between foreign and domestic economic policy have become so blurred that each flows into the other. What any state and every central bank may do at home will affect other states and banks as well, intentionally or unintentionally. There is no such thing anymore as domestic economic policy, especially for a major country. Global financial markets now link all macroeconomic policies into a common net, with traders everywhere generating ripple effects for every government and central bank action. Global commercial markets are equally pervasive, and those that exclude themselves from competition do so at their long-term peril. There can be no such thing anymore as an isolated currency or an isolated economy.

This creates new pressures on governments and on producers. A state that wants to compete internationally has to conduct appropriate policies at home. A state that wants prosperity at home has to follow certain policies abroad. States cannot coordinate their global economic policies without adjusting their domestic policies as well. Every producer must recognize that his company's current and potential competitors are everywhere, and that he cannot hope to escape or to exclude them over the long run. And every producer must think about foreign as well as domestic markets.

Governments regard this new net of interactions with ambivalence. They do not relish being affected by the policies of others, especially when those policies are based on different philosophies and on different policy objectives. They want to be able to make their own decisions, especially because those decisions can affect their own political fortunes very directly. They do not want to have their economic cycles determined by others. If they cannot avoid the impact of foreign actions on their own economies, they at least want to have some influence on those others and to block policies that will jeopardize their own prosperity. They do not like being exposed and perhaps vulnerable.

Governments and central banks also feel uncomfortable about market instabilities. They want to avoid having their currencies, their securities, or their exchange rates buffeted by the actions of others or by the effects of contradictory policies. This reinforces their determination to coordinate their economic policies, and it has led to the establishment of a global economic system radically different from those that existed before World Wars I and II. In fact, one of the principal responsibilities of the global concert has been to coordinate economic policies and to overcome the market effects of frequent failures to coordinate.

Governments also feel uncomfortable about the effects of a free trading system. Such a system subjects an economy to the constant strain of competition. It is also hideously difficult to bring about truly free trade, as the possibilities for abuse are almost endless. Every producer and trader believes that others have one kind of advantage or another, and those producers and traders are constantly attempting to persuade their governments that they deserve their government's support to protect them from the abuses of others. There is often enough substance behind those claims to warrant investigation and perhaps some form of intervention, but much of the time there is none or very little.

The first effort to establish a new international financial and monetary system took place during World War II, when the major states of what was then the global concert met at the New Hampshire resort of Bretton Woods. They founded a structure based on the U.S. dollar and on a firm link ($35 per troy ounce) between the dollar and gold. The system functioned effectively for two decades but broke down when the divergences between different governments and central banks—especially the German and the American—became too great. The U.S. government cut the dollar-gold link in 1971, largely because German economic policies made the Deutsche mark—or the D-mark—consistently stronger than the dollar. Washington wanted Germany to revalue the D-Mark upwards, but when the German government refused to contemplate revaluation the American government in effect devalued the dollar. Despite this breakdown of the Bretton Woods system, efforts at international macroeconomic coordination actually intensified to compensate.

The international trading system was established after the monetary system. It was created by the United States and other states of the global concert in 1947 at Havana, Cuba, through the General Agreement on Tariffs and Trade (GATT), which generally provided for a liberal international trading regime based on the "most favored nation" principle. Under this principle, any state that grants a trade concession to one other state must also provide it to any other state. The Havana agreement, which gave rise to the GATT organization, has not broken down but has actually expanded over the decades since World War II. Through a series of negotiating rounds, usually named either after a place or a person (such as the

Tokyo Round or the Kennedy Round), different areas of commerce have been pulled into the system. The current round, initiated in 1986 at Punta del Este and therefore termed the Uruguay Round, was intended to bring trade in agriculture, services, and intellectual property into the system. It has floundered, largely because of difficulties over agricultural trade, and has repeatedly had to be extended well after its original 1990 deadline.

After the collapse of the Bretton Woods financial and monetary system, the U.S. government convened an informal gathering that was known as the Library Group, a small circle of five countries named after its first meeting in the White House library. Germany and the United States were in that group (which later came to be known as the Group of Five or the G-5), along with France, Great Britain, and Japan—the key members of the new global concert. Later, Canada and Italy joined to form the G-7. The G-7 finance ministers and central bankers still meet frequently and consult around the clock. Their chiefs of government hold annual summit meetings. The 1992 gathering was held in Munich and the 1993 meeting, in Tokyo. The G-7 have tried to guide exchange rates or at least to moderate swings, and they have also attempted to coordinate their general fiscal, monetary, and trade policies. All too often, and increasingly in the 1990s, they have been unable to coordinate their policies and they have merely coordinated their market interventions.

The United States and Germany, often the two largest exporting states in the world and two of the three most important economies, have placed particular stress on trying to coordinate their policies and those of others. Any policies on which they can agree are likely to set the tone for the entire global economic system and the terms of economic security for all. Both are acutely aware that it was the divergence between West German and American monetary policies that brought about the collapse of the Bretton Woods system, and that no global system can function unless the United States and Germany agree to participate even if they do not agree to pursue identical policies.

With the end of the cold war, therefore, the economic element may well become the most important foundation for German-American relations and a crucial element in their cooperation. It can be as important as their defense collaboration was during the cold war. It could become the basic engine of the relationship, and the one by which the relationship might stand or fall.

In principle, German-American economic coordination should be readily achievable. Germany and the United States have important common economic interests. They both have a free market system. They also want and need an open global trading system, despite domestic pressures for protection and despite their worries about the competition from Japan and others. Both want smooth and steady exchange rate relationships. Both also want a mutual understanding on domestic short-term interest rate policies. Neither wants to repeat the cycles of competitive devaluation and protection which helped lead to the Great Depression, and neither wants a financial crisis.

Despite these common interests, however, German-American economic coordination can become not only the most important but also the most problematic
part of the relationship. It has remained consistently elusive and has recently become more difficult. Discussions about financial and commercial policy have
generated German-American arguments, some of them quite acrimonious, even
during the cold war. They can generate even greater arguments in future.

ECONOMIC PHILOSOPHIES AND
MACROECONOMIC POLICIES

The United States and Germany have virtually opposite economic philosophies,
doctrines, traditions and attitudes. They pursue different monetary and industrial policies and they see the economic world very differently.

The American government and the U.S. Federal Reserve Bank generally follow
Keynesian concepts of fiscal demand management as well as monetary stimula-
tion principles, although the U.S. government has lost control of its fiscal processes since 1974 when the U.S. Congress assumed full authority over the budget.
The German government, and especially the Bundesbank, concentrate their efforts on achieving stability as their main policy goal. American interest rates
will rise and fall more sharply than German rates, and the risk of inflation in the
United States will be greater. Over time, the contrasting German and American
monetary attitudes and policies have made the D-Mark one of the strongest currencies in the world and particularly strong with respect to the dollar. Since
World War II the D-mark has lost less of its value than has any other major currency and has more than doubled in value with respect to the U.S. dollar.

Germany and the United States pursue different industrial strategies and practices. The Americans stress economic liberalism in the traditional English sense.
The Germans follow long-standing continental practices of cooperation between
government, industry, and labor. In Germany, government and industry see each
other as friends and partners; in the United States, they often see each other as
enemies.

German industry pursues a more conservative philosophy than does American
industry. The most important German industries have existed for generations, as
have most of the major German industrial concerns. German industry pursues incre-
mental productivity growth in established production lines. It stresses high quality
and reliable service, making the demand for certain German products such as machine tools virtually inelastic. German labor, like German industry, likes continuity;
the highly trained German workers prefer to remain in their chosen industrial
or service professions for life. They do not want to be relocated for restructuring or
retraining. To avoid some of the changes that might be dictated by global competition, portions of German industry—like other European industry—are preserved,
subsidized, and sometimes sheltered directly or through the EC. But other portions
are highly competitive and dominate their fields.

American production, by contrast, is in almost constant upheaval, although some of it is also subsidized and protected, if to a lesser degree. There is a high premium on growth, on innovation, on the development of new processes and of entire new industries or new agricultural techniques. Americans are more prepared than Germans to accept the social costs of industrial advance and disruption. American industries and enterprises are much more likely to rise and fall. Labor, less well trained, is often more flexible, and it has a much lower level of commitment to existing industries, plants or processes. Americans have during the decade of the 1980s created and developed entire industries—such as computers—that are barely launched in Germany, and the United States is constantly in the forefront of technological exploration and innovation, while the Germans excel at perfecting traditional production lines. Where German advances are gradual, American processes often appear and sometimes are chaotic.

The American system suffers much more than the German from competing centers of economic authority and power. There are three separate economic sovereignties in Washington: the Federal Reserve Bank, the president's administration, and the Congress. The president and the Congress rarely agree on economic policy or on fiscal policy, even when they are of the same political party. They generate budget deficits because each has favorite programs that it wants to finance. Individual members of Congress also often pursue policies designed to favor the commercial interests of producers from their districts. The Federal Reserve attempts to reduce the impact of disagreements between the administration and the Congress on the currency markets and also attempts to manage the dollar. Each often goes its own way.

In Germany, the cabinet and the Bundestag are under the control of the same political party or parties, although the Bundesrat may be under different control. The government and the Bundesbank are often in broad agreement even when there are differences about specific policies. For example, during 1991 the Bundesbank raised short-term interest rates immediately after the German government had agreed in a G-7 meeting that interest rates should remain stable. Later reports suggested that the president of the Bundesbank, Helmut Schlesinger, had been out-voted by the regional bank chiefs. But such disagreements pale in comparison with the long-standing incapacity of the U.S. administration and Congress to manage a common budget. Even the Germans most sympathetic to the United States have given up trying to understand American fiscal and monetary policies.

The two economies also have very different orientations. The German economy is export-oriented. One-third of the West German gross domestic product (GDP) went into exports during the latter half of the 1980s, with about one-half of all trade being with the European Community and another quarter being with other West European states. An almost equal proportion of East German GDP was exported, with one-half going to the Soviet Union. Although all these proportions have declined under the demands of German unification, they reflect the concentrated export effort at which German managers excel. By contrast, only about one-tenth of the American GDP is exported. West Germany was the world's largest exporter in 1988. Because of its larger GDP, the United States was the world's largest exporter in 1989. In 1990, united Germany won that title, and in 1991 America won again. Japan consistently placed third.

German prosperity therefore depends heavily on foreign demand. American prosperity depends heavily on domestic demand. Germany must concentrate on maintaining international competitiveness. The United States must concentrate on maintaining domestic markets. Germany will want to pursue monetary and fiscal policies that keep costs down through consistently low inflation and low long-term interest rates. The United States is more ready to permit short-term interest rate swings, attempting alternately to expand growth quickly and then to curtail potentially resulting inflation in its own version of Keynesian macroeconomic policy. Each serves and targets its chosen market.

With the gradual expansion of the European Community, Germany has become increasingly unable to conduct a fully independent economic policy. Many German-American economic differences, especially in trade, can no longer be solved bilaterally.

As the European Community has consolidated, and as the Community has adopted and largely carried out its EC 1992 single-market concept, German commercial policy is increasingly made in Brussels. The German government can no longer set its own trading principles and tariffs or its own commercial rules and industrial regulations. Such matters are now decided by the EC Council of Ministers and the EC Commission, and it is difficult for Germany to override other EC members except in very urgent cases where a major German national interest is directly at stake. A great deal of current German economic and industrial legislation and regulation, as in other EC countries, is designed to implement EC Commission policies.

German monetary policy is directed toward managing the European as well as the German economy. The European Community in 1979 established the European Monetary System (EMS) and its subsidiary European Exchange Rate Mechanism (ERM) under which a growing number of EC nations have fixed their exchange rates to each other and especially to the German D-mark. Further, the EC heads of state and government agreed at the Maastricht summit in December 1991 to establish a European Monetary Union (EMU) by 1997 or at the latest by January 1, 1999. The EMU will be under the control of a European central bank closely modeled on the German Bundesbank but with an international board. Until that time, however, European monetary policy will continue to be largely set by the Bundesbank, as many major European currencies remain tied to the D-mark.

The Bundesbank thus has to think in terms of managing a continental, not a national, currency, and it has to make certain that the currency is strong enough that no outside holder will cause a run on the currency by wanting to sell it. The Bundesbank is now and will in future be Europe's central bank in reality even if the Maastricht agreements are not implemented as originally agreed because of resistance from some European countries (as in the first Danish referendum of May, 1992). For the German central bank, therefore, Europe is now much more important in many ways than the United States.

Because of the importance that it attaches to European exchange rate stability as a prelude to the arrival of the European Monetary Union, the Bundesbank will lean toward relatively restrictive policies during most of the decade. Since 1990, the bank has already had to become more restrictive because it has wanted to offset the fiscal stimulus of large German budget deficits used to finance unification. The successor European central bank—if fully established by the end of the 1990s—will be under significant German influence. It will also have to lean toward restrictive and anti-inflationary policies in order to establish its credibility early and especially in Germany. Thus, unless there is a major global recession or depression during the 1990s, German (and thus European) monetary policy is likely to remain relatively restrictive during much of the decade.

Such policies are almost certain to generate German-American debates and disputes during the 1990s. The American government has complained about what it has regarded as restrictive German monetary policy during most of the postwar period. Those complaints have rarely led to changes in German policy and are even less likely to do so during the coming decade. German-American policy differences and arguments have not always disrupted the international system in the past, largely because the two states and other G-7 members have been able to coordinate market interventions even if they could not coordinate their policies. In fact, the market interventions were often needed in order to offset the effects of German and American conflicting policies.

In the future, however, the differences between fundamental German and American economic and monetary doctrines, attitudes, and policies can have much more serious consequences. German policies will have a more powerful effect because they will shape the macroeconomic policies and exchange rates of other European currencies through the EMS-ERM and the process of moving toward EMU. Moreover, the long-term boom of the 1980s has ended and the U.S. government is watching even minor economic fluctuations with much more attention than before. The G-7 mechanism has failed to coordinate respective German and American policies and has been most often used in order to coordinate the timing of interventions needed to offset the differences in policy.

If German policies keep all of Europe in a long-term economic slowdown, they will have a global as well as a national and a continental effect. The American government, attempting to pull out of the 1990–1992 recession, has already expressed some irritation at the limits that the Bundesbank's policies placed on U.S. freedom of maneuver. At the July, 1992, Munich summit of the G-7, U.S. Treasury secretary James Brady tried repeatedly to persuade German finance minister Theo Waigel to urge the Bundesbank to ease monetary policy, but Waigel and Kohl strongly supported the bank. In fact, German monetary policy hardened further after the summit, to the point where German as well as other European business firms began to express serious concern and the dollar began weakening to ever lower levels against the D-mark.

This dialogue has not changed materially during the Clinton administration. The American government has consistently wanted the Bundesbank to lower short-term interest rates in order to stimulate the European economies and help U.S. exports to Europe. And the Bundesbank has remained as obdurate as in the past, stressing that its policies are precisely in reaction to the profligacy of governments. Even when the bank began lowering its short-term interest rates during early 1993, it obviously did so in reaction to domestic and European considerations, not because of American pressures, and it did so at a pace that left the Americans frustrated about their inability to export more to a Europe that would remain in recession because of the Bundesbank's policies.

The U.S. government is bound to complain about this even more in future, for the difference in policies reflects a fundamental difference in economic and monetary philosophy and not some passing disagreement that was exacerbated by U.S. election year politics. The European effect makes the issue more serious but does not change the basic problem. German-American differences helped to bring down the Bretton Woods system, and they can cause more serious crises now when Germany's weight is greater than before.

The policy pursued by the Bundesbank contributed to a crisis in the European Exchange Rate Mechanism in the autumn of 1992. The recession that was developing in Germany and several other European countries at the time threatened to become even more serious, thus threatening a cut in American exports and a further slowdown of the American recovery.

Beyond Europe, the increase in German power and influence exercises a broadly disinflationary pressure across the global economy as a whole. Some, including many Americans, complain that its effect is actually deflationary. Others, however, believe that the Bundesbank is right and that American policies designed to stimulate demand at different times—often in conjunction with American electoral cycles—have jeopardized not only American but also global monetary stability and have consistently increased the risk of global inflation. By that reckoning, the widening of German monetary influence across Europe and across the world as a whole can be seen as a healthy development which increases the prospects of long-lasting global stability.

There is, however, a price to be paid. The Bundesbank, through the EMS-ERM connection, has already forced changes in the policies of many West European governments. Even if those governments have been glad to accept the changes because they have welcomed the stability that an association with the D-mark can bring, the Europeans are now facing the recessionary pressures brought on because the Bundesbank is trying to impose greater discipline in Germany itself. In effect, Western Europe suffers recession because of German unification policies.

This message was not lost on the United States during 1992. The Federal

Reserve Bank had been attempting to fight inflation but did not want to jeopardize the chances for the reelection of President Bush. It had been reducing short-term interest rates in order to bring the country out of recession. The U.S. discount rate dropped from 7 percent to 3 percent during the years from 1990 to 1992, but the German Lombard rate rose from 8 percent to above 10 percent during the same period. This restricted the U.S. government's ability to stimulate its own economy. Europe may be ready to accept the results of German policies, but the United States is not—even if those policies might exercise a useful corrective to the excesses of the American system.

Americans must face another potential long-term problem, one that is still only a vague shadow on the horizon but that can become very serious over time. As German economic power and influence increase, the capacity of the American government and of the Federal Reserve to manipulate U.S. demand cycles will be materially diminished. The D-mark is already the world's second-largest reserve currency, at over 20 percent of global monetary reserves. It will not soon reach or exceed the U.S. level of over 50 percent, but it has been rising steadily. The real story of the postwar years, and one that is little recognized in the United States, is not the rise in Japanese but the rise in German economic power and influence.

If these trends continue, the Americans will need to recognize that they can no longer raise and lower interest rates as flexibly as in the past, for the D-mark offers a credible alternative if the U.S. dollar begins to lose its attractiveness. Over time, the rising influence of the D-mark, and of German economic policy, can force changes not only in immediate American policy but in the entire American concept of demand management.

These are long-term trends, but they have an inexorable force. The U.S. government will not lightly accept the decline in its own independence on matters that are of considerable financial and even political importance. It will be more ready than European governments to object strenuously to German actions and policies. German macroeconomic policy risks becoming an ever more bitter bone of contention between Germany and the United States.

TRADE AND THE GATT

Another issue, however, has dominated the German-American dialogue much more during the late 1980s and early 1990s. It is potentially more important than the long-standing divergence in monetary policy, for it can affect the survival of the international trading system which the United States and the other states of the global concert established after World War II and which has helped Germany as much as any other nation.

The issue that might provoke the greatest conflict between German and American policies is protectionism. Both the United States and the European Community have increasingly slid into protectionist practices during the 1980s, although they have been able to maintain the broad framework of international cooperation under the international trading regime of the GATT. But they have for several years been unable to agree on ways to advance that regime through further negotiations, and the failure to achieve a successful outcome to those negotiations could powerfully strengthen protectionist tendencies on both sides of the Atlantic.

The negotiations, being conducted within the framework of the Uruguay Round, were to be completed years ago. They have had to be extended several times because of difficulties in reaching agreement on several thorny issues, but especially because of sharp complaints by the United States and other agricultural exporting states against the EC system of agricultural production and export subsidies known as the Common Agricultural Policy (CAP). Those subsidies have cut into agricultural exports from the United States, Australia, Argentina, and other farming nations that have formed their own circle, designated as the Cairns Group. The EC has also dumped cheap food on world markets in ways that have helped undercut the development efforts of Third World nations. The United States and the other food-exporting states have been demanding a substantial reduction in those subsidies and in particular a cut in EC agricultural export subsidies, with the European states resisting firmly. France, Western Europe's largest food exporter, has been adamantly opposed to the level of export reductions being demanded by the United States and other members of the Cairns Group.

German-American relations can be severely damaged if the Uruguay Round fails. This was a special problem for President Bush, who believed that he had a firm commitment from Chancellor Kohl that Kohl would make the negotiations succeed. According to U.S. officials, the chancellor told President Bush during the Houston G-7 summit in 1990 that he would intervene personally to solve the problem. American officials interpreted that to mean that Kohl would persuade French president François Mitterrand to accept changes in the CAP. But nothing further happened during 1990 and 1991, in part because of German and French elections. The meeting between Bush and Kohl at Camp David in March 1992 brought no progress and left Bush with no time to solve the problem before he had to face his own farmers for reelection in the politically vital American Middle West.

With lack of agreement on agricultural issues stalling the momentum of the negotiations, other matters have also begun to look more difficult. Several partners to the negotiations have begun to harden their positions across the board. Questions that had once seemed solvable—like services and intellectual property rules—have begun to pose major problems.

As the talks have dragged on, the mood between American and German officials has also worsened.

- The Americans have complained that the Germans are inconsistent, with Bonn officials asserting repeatedly that the Uruguay Round must be brought to a successful conclusion but then doing little to force progress and only telling the Americans to deal with the European Commission in Brussels. The Americans have long believed that Brussels is excessively subject to French influence, an impression that was reinforced when EC Commission president Jacques Delors in March 1992 summarily rejected a proposal from President Bush with the statement that he was not empowered to negotiate and that Bush should have worked out the issues with Kohl. At the Munich G-7 summit, Bush was again urged to talk to Delors and the meeting proved equally fruitless.

- The Germans have said that they genuinely want to solve the trade problem but that their hands are tied. They have complained that the Americans appear to believe that Germany must be the American stalking horse in the Community, a task that the Germans have said they cannot and will not undertake. They also argue that Franco-German cooperation is an essential foundation for a united Europe—an objective that the United States should support. Some Germans have added privately that the Americans should not press so hard, that the CAP is doomed to collapse from its own weight because of the sheer cost of subsidies, and that the United States and other food-exporting states will get what they want in due course.

Chancellor Kohl, however, has also faced complaints from German industry and labor that the EC farm subsidies are jeopardizing Germany's trading position around the world. German industry and German trade unions had even sent him a joint letter to express their demand for a successful conclusion of the Uruguay Round. The chancellor therefore instructed the former German minister of agriculture, Ignaz Kiechle, to negotiate a revision of the CAP, and by the latter part of May in 1992 the EC had taken a number of steps to that end. Kohl himself presumably notified Mitterrand that he had changed his views and the instructions he had given his minister.

After a typical all-night meeting that culminated a three-day negotiating session, the EC farm ministers on May 21 agreed to a cut of 29 percent in cereal subsidies as well as other subsidies by 1996. They agreed to revise the system for calculating farm subsidies so as to remove incentives for over-production. They also agreed that EC farmers would be compensated for taking 15 percent of their land out of production, a plan that should reduce the European food mountains that have in the past helped force European states to export food at virtually any price. Finally, they also agreed to a general reduction in EC agricultural exports.

American officials and negotiators, as well as other members of the Cairns Group, welcomed the EC actions but warned that they did not go far enough to meet all U.S. concerns. According to the United States, the EC ministers did not sufficiently reduce export levels. The Americans also fear that the EC agreement might not genuinely cut into production as much as the EC negotiators believed they will, for farmers will always take out their least productive land.

Nonetheless, the U.S. government welcomed the change in EC attitudes, and the negotiating round resumed with greater prospects for success. As a sign that President Bush was personally interested in the prospects for the Uruguay Round, Secretary Baker attended the first European-American negotiating session after the new EC policy had been announced. And differences on several contentious issues were significantly narrowed, although not eliminated.

The G-7 discussion of the Uruguay Round in Munich did not yield any concrete results. Chancellor Kohl did not want to put the issue on the agenda because he did not want a contentious discussion, but President Bush and Secretary Baker proceeded to raise it at several opportunities. British prime minister John Major, who was then president of the EC Council, supported Bush. But, although differences between American and EC negotiators had narrowed, no agreement could be reached at the Munich summit.

As the Munich summit ended, the U.S. government proceeded to conclude an agreement with Canada and Mexico creating a North American Free Trade Area (NAFTA). In effect, Bush decided that he would be prepared to favor regional trade agreements if the global agreement no longer served American needs. Thus, the frequent delays in the Uruguay Round risked jeopardizing the entire GATT structure.

One thing was also strikingly clear. After the Munich summit, Bush was not prepared to give Chancellor Kohl any credit for a GATT breakthrough. More likely, Bush would appreciate whatever Major might do to bring about progress or success. The bitterness over the GATT failure undoubtedly contributed to Bush's decision not even to attempt to visit Bonn on his return from Moscow in January of 1993.

President Clinton has advanced further in the same direction that President Bush began. He said frequently during his campaign for president that it might be good to have regional trade agreements, and he proceeded immediately after his election to indicate his support for the NAFTA accord with some amendments. His trade negotiators were clearly interested in resuming the Uruguay Round negotiations after he and they took office in early 1993, but he did not signal the kind of urgency that Bush had shown. In his inaugural address, Clinton gave the impression that he regarded Germany and the European Community as competitors, whatever common interests they might also have as allies. Europeans might find that agreement with Clinton is harder to reach than it would have been with Bush.

The evolution of the Uruguay Round, however, is only one part—albeit a very sensitive one—of the broad problem that German-American relations will face over trade during the next several years. For the differences between the two economies and their production styles are now showing themselves in major divergences between the two economies, and it will be more difficult in the future to negotiate solutions that compensate for these divergences.

The U.S. economy, chaotic as it is, has been spewing forth new products and services at an almost unprecedented pace. It is American industry, together with Japanese industry, that is now leading the technological revolution in the world.

German industry, like European industry as a whole, has been unable to sustain the pace, although individual German firms have kept the lead in some specific areas. The European Community Council and the Commission have been targeting specific high-technology areas for industrial policy, attempting to create a European technological revolution, but the successes for this policy have been few and far between. Most European high-technology fairs, whether in computer or communications systems, are dominated by American and Japanese products.

German firms, like other European Community firms, have also increasingly become high-cost producers. German wages and social costs have climbed to the point where the cost of labor in Germany is the highest in the world. In Europe, where the economy is seen not only in terms of production but also in terms of social welfare, such costs have created no problem and have been part of the norm—at least in the most industrialized and richest states. The ever-rising standard of living and of social well-being was part of the struggle against Communism. But when this rise has also been linked to such a strong currency as the D-Mark, they can prove to be a handicap in global competition.

In the United States, wages and capital costs have been declining even as they have been rising in Europe. Over ten million legal immigrants arrived during the 1980s, and two million more have been admitted since then. These numbers are larger than for the 1900–1910 period, which had been the record decade to date. Many of the new immigrants are of non-European origin. They are generating political and economic problems, but they also represent an inflow of labor that has kept American wages and prices relatively low in many areas and that has provided a genuine stimulus for some sectors of the American economy. Despite the problems of economic management that are all too apparent in Washington, many industries in the United States have become more aggressive and competitive.

These twin developments form the basis for more German-American or European-American trade disputes, as well as for increasing European refusals to accept American and Japanese high-technology products. For European industry risks pricing itself out of world markets unless it can find ways to lower its costs. It may also continue to fall further behind in the most modern areas of production. Germany does not suffer these effects as much as do some other European nations, but it may also decide that it will need more sheltering in the future than in the past. That sheltering may take the form not only of price protection but also of technological protection.

The problems arise at both ends. There are ever greater pressures for protection in the United States, and the Clinton administration appears to be heeding at least some of them. The European Community will face similar pressures, for it must defend itself not only against the United States and Japan but also against the East European producers in basic industries, textiles, and agriculture who have lower operating costs. The demands for change in the global trading system can become increasingly difficult to resist.

American and German officials and economists warn that the world will increasingly move toward "managed trade," in which different states will sign bilateral or limited multilateral trade agreements rather than continuing to function under the universal system of the GATT. Such managed trade has been tried or is being tried in automobiles, computer chips, and aircraft. Some believe that it may be possible to negotiate better terms through separate agreements. The EC and Japan have been attempting to do that. Such separate arrangements would not, however, be to either America's or Germany's long-term advantage. Germany would be even more seriously hurt because of its greater dependence on exports and because it could not negotiate a trade surplus as impressive as that which its exporters are able to achieve in an open-market system.

The GATT argument, like the debate about economic coordination and even about monetary policy, thus points to a much more fundamental issue for both Germany and the United States, which is the future organization of the world economy. The governing system since the 1940s has been essentially an American system, created and expanded during and after World War II largely under U.S. leadership. It reflects American thinking and American practices as well as the needs of the global concert. It has helped America and Germany not only by lowering worldwide production costs but also by increasing global prosperity.

With protectionist pressures rising and with dim prospects for true coordination of monetary policy, Germany and the United States have to decide whether they wish to continue to preserve that system or whether they wish to replace it with something different. The G-7 meetings, instead of exchanging polite platitudes about common well-being and positive expectations, should perhaps begin to address these kinds of questions or at least begin to contemplate the alternatives.

The coordination of German-American economic policy, whether on trade or monetary issues, thus looms as a thorny and probably contentious question that will complicate relations continually and probably increasingly. It will require constant attention and careful management, particularly because the objective conditions of the two economies are now diverging and their monetary needs are also doing so. But Bonn, Frankfurt, and Washington need to find some kind of agreement, for in economic policy there can be no truly separate path. The temptation to find one may be great, but it does not truly exist.

10

MILITARY COOPERATION

German-American military relations have changed more suddenly and more dramatically than every other element of the relationship. For almost forty years, military cooperation was the single most important consideration in the German-American alliance. It gave both nations a sense of security that they could not have had with any other partner. It also preserved the peace of Europe and of the world. Now that the cold war is over and both states appear to believe that they no longer need each other, attitudes and policies are being fundamentally changed—especially in Germany.

German-American military cooperation had a very clear and sharply definable purpose: to defend West German and West European territory against a possible Soviet attack, and to make that defense so powerful and persuasive that no attack would ever come. This was not only a German-American purpose but the key objective of the entire North Atlantic alliance.

The U.S. government began to worry about the protection of its own occupation zone in Germany even before the Federal Republic of Germany was established as a state. During the Berlin Blockade, the American occupation commander, General Lucius Clay, once informed Washington that he feared a possible Soviet attack and a war in Germany. Although others were not sure that he was right, the U.S. government understood the importance even then of keeping the Western sectors of Berlin and the Western occupation zones of Germany out of Soviet hands.

The U.S. government at first felt confident that American atomic bombs would deter Soviet aggression, but the North Korean attack against South Korea in June 1950 made many Americans and Germans fear that the Soviets might try to launch a similar attack in Europe. American force deployments in German grew to meet and thereby to forestall such a threat. But, as U.S. and non-German West European forces were not ever likely to grow to a number that could match the Soviet army, the U.S. government began to favor German rearmament as part of the North Atlantic Treaty Organization (NATO). Separate German rearmament came about in 1955 after abortive proposals for a common European defense force, and the new West German army was given the task of helping to defend the NATO border in Central Europe.

From 1955 to 1990, when Germany was reunited, West German and American troops shared the principal responsibility for the defense of the border between East and West Germany. Other NATO forces were also involved, but West German forces and American forces were assigned to defend the most sensitive portions of the border. This defense was the dominant element of their relationship, especially for Germany. It was so important to both countries that they could not permit other problems to interfere with it, and it compelled them to solve those other problems to avoid damage to their military alliance.

That alliance saw the defense of West Germany not as an isolated objective but as part of the struggle to preserve the global balance of power. In case of a Soviet/ Warsaw Pact attack, Germans would be fighting for their land, but they and the Americans and other allies would also be fighting to keep Western Europe as a whole out of Soviet hands and thus also to keep Western Europe in the global system. Recognizing what was at stake, the United States usually kept around a quarter of a million troops in Germany, and the Germans had an armed force of almost half a million. About 150,000 other NATO forces also helped defend West Germany. After 1955 they were true comrades in arms, which would not have been conceivable in 1945.

NATO defense plans also included about 7,000 U.S. nuclear weapons deployed in Europe, with perhaps half in Germany, as well as the backing of the U.S. strategic nuclear arsenal. The tactical nuclear weapons, and the very real possibility that they might have to be detonated on German soil—East or West—constituted one of the most painful issues between Bonn and Washington as well as within NATO as a whole. NATO doctrine was based on the presence of such weapons and on a commitment to use them, if necessary before the Soviet Union did. Moreover, the American intercontinental ballistic arsenal also stood ready for use if necessary. It was this commitment that gave Germany a defense to a depth it could not have achieved by any other means.

West Germany and the United States did not want to fight a war but to deter it. Both governments wanted to make absolutely clear that any invasion of West Germany would lead to fierce retaliation, perhaps intercontinental, against the Soviet Union and those who joined it. The American government, which wanted Moscow to have no illusion about U.S. determination to protect West Germany, established a complex command and control system which would ensure that American nuclear forces stood ready to retaliate no matter what form the Soviet attack might take.

The threat of nuclear retaliation sometimes frightened the West German public, as well as the American, almost as much as the risk of war itself. The Soviet and East German governments used this to press the West for a declaration that NATO would not be first to use nuclear weapons, but neither the American nor the West German government yielded to those pressures. American critics of NATO plans also used to complain that the potential engagement of U.S. intercontinental nuclear weapons might put Chicago at risk in order to save Berlin, but American and NATO planners replied that the Soviet government would only be deterred if Moscow understood that U.S. intercontinental weapons would be used and that the United States would be totally engaged and totally committed. NATO became an important part of Germany's return to international respectability and acceptance. Great Britain's Lord Ismay, NATO's first secretary general, reportedly said that NATO had been created to keep the Russians out, the Americans in, and the Germans down. NATO achieved the two first missions but it did not achieve the third. The Germans did rise, to the point where the current NATO secretary general is a German, Manfred Wörner. In fact, NATO turned out to be precisely the vehicle by which Germany could rise, because others needed a German role in the defense of Europe as much as the Germans needed their support. Moreover, the close military cooperation, and the many personal friendships cemented in NATO headquarters and between allied and German military and civilians, formed a backbone of mutual understanding that helped to overcome or at least to ease the memories of two world wars.

The immense American deployment in turn permitted Germany to be secure and to return to power without appearing to threaten any other state. When NATO was formed and when the NATO allies and the West German government decided that West Germany needed an army, the common joke was that the German army would have to be strong enough to frighten the Soviets but not the Belgians. The U.S. presence, like the German membership in NATO, squared the circle, helping to protect West Germany without making it necessary for Bonn to recruit an overwhelming force that might intimidate its smaller Western neighbors and revive the fear of Germany, a fear that remained a constant element in Western Europe for decades after the war.

The German-American military partnership established the great high arch of the transatlantic alliance, an arch that reached from one pedestal in the heartland of the United States to another in the Federal Republic. That arch joined the NATO forces in Germany and the U.S. nuclear deterrent, as well as all the many forces that lay between, into a common strategic plan and into a common deterrent. Berliners could walk in safety along the Kurfürstendamm and picnic in the Grunwald—even though they were surrounded by twenty hostile divisions—because American nuclear-tipped missiles were stationed in silos throughout the American West and deep below the open seas.

German membership in NATO and in the defense of Europe gave the global concert its solid foothold on the European continent. It was the European leg of the global tripod. It remained strong and unchallengeable throughout the years of the cold war, providing a firm basis for the global concert's position in Europe and also for German membership in that concert. For the first time in its history, Germany had a powerful role in a global alliance system instead of one in opposition to such a system.

Despite their common strategic interests, their common membership in the global alliance, and their close cooperation, the German and American governments and military staffs often argued about military doctrine and tactics. In particular, they differed on how to make clear to Moscow that the defense of Germany and the United States was firmly linked. This linkage, known as "coupling," served as the main deterrent. If it came into question, the German government feared, Moscow might theoretically be tempted to attack. But because the concept was ephemeral, Bonn and Washington often disagreed about how to achieve it. The German government always wanted the American commitment to be absolute and unquestionable, because any doubts might tempt a Soviet attack. The U.S. government agreed, but it periodically altered its strategy and occasionally did not deal with German fears as fast or as fully as Bonn wanted.

During the 1950s, Chancellor Konrad Adenauer and the German government supported the American concept of "massive retaliation" introduced by Secretary of State John Foster Dulles and President Dwight Eisenhower because it clearly committed the United States to protect German territory by global nuclear war. When President John Kennedy and Secretary of Defense Robert McNamara decided that massive retaliation was no longer credible once the Soviet Union had large numbers of atomic bombs, they shifted to "flexible response."

Adenauer objected to the new U.S. policy, fearing that flexibility would be interpreted as a sign that the United States lacked determination, especially after the United States had not challenged the building of the Berlin Wall in August, 1961. French president Charles de Gaulle took advantage of the Bonn-Washington debate and of Adenauer's doubts about the United States to draw West Germany closer to France.

In part to ease that particular argument, and in part to give Germany a stronger voice in alliance strategic councils, Washington proposed giving West Germany an important role—and even potentially a nuclear role—by creating a "multilateral force" (MLF) that would include German soldiers with other allied forces, but the idea generated so much misunderstanding and opposition (including in Germany) that President Lyndon Johnson withdrew it. Instead, West Germany was given a permanent seat on the newly created Nuclear Planning Group (NPG), which satisfied Bonn's desire to have a voice in alliance nuclear strategy without raising fears of German nuclear weapons.

Other debates followed. When Jimmy Carter was U.S. president, he proposed the deployment of so-called neutron bombs, enhanced-radiation warheads with high radiation output compared to blast, but the Western press denounced the warheads as "the ultimate capitalist weapon" because they could kill persons even in areas where the bomb blast had relatively limited destructive effect on build-ings and other structures. After intense domestic debate and violent controversy in West Germany, Chancellor Helmut Schmidt agreed to the deployment of the weapons on German soil. Then Carter changed his mind, leaving Schmidt isolated, furious, and weakened domestically.

Later, in October 1977, Chancellor Schmidt initiated another alliance debate when he warned that the Soviet deployment of a new medium-range mobile nuclear missile, the SS-20, could undercut NATO deterrence doctrine because it would intimidate all of Europe. President Carter very reluctantly agreed to deploy new American intermediate nuclear forces (INF), such as Pershing-II and cruise missiles, to neutralize the Soviet buildup. Before the U.S. and NATO deployment actually took place, more than five years later, Schmidt himself had fallen from power, leaving the final deployment and a fierce German domestic debate to Chancellor Helmut Kohl and President Ronald Reagan.

As this review shows, German-American debates about strategy and tactics were always resolved. Neither Bonn nor Washington had any other possible choice. Only the United States could deter a possible Soviet attack on Germany and Berlin, and only West Germany would give the U.S. armed forces the kind of European continental base that America needed to be a credible world power and that the global concert needed to act in Europe. No matter how heated the German-American debates might be, they ended with agreement and with compromises that suited both the German and American governments and publics. They were also usually resolved not bilaterally but in the multilateral surroundings of NATO, for the German-American military relationship was only part of the entire NATO complex. In fact, the existence of the multilateral NATO structure often made it possible to solve bilateral disagreements.

The German-American ability to cooperate in defense matters, even under severe pressure, made an impression in Moscow as well. The successful deployment of the Pershings and the cruise missiles showed that a further Soviet military buildup could not overcome NATO's determination to maintain a European balance and could not destroy the German-American link. Moscow finally had no option except to find a new European policy, and that new policy led to the dismantling of the Soviet imperium.

The Eastern military threat to West Germany ended in 1990 and 1991 with German unification, the demise of the Warsaw Pact, and the disintegration of the Soviet Union. The Soviet forces that remain in Eastern Germany are to be withdrawn by the fall of 1994. They often seem a pathetic remnant of a great army, huddled in their barracks and trying to make money by selling their uniforms and equipment. They are not now regarded as a serious military threat even if their presence represents a potential Soviet lever on German policy and remains a sensitive issue for the German government. There is, therefore, no more perceived danger either of Soviet invasion or nuclear attack, and no more need for the kind of defense that NATO established.

NEW THREATS

The new threats are less clear and less easily definable. Nor are they controllable or preventable by the kind of deterrence policy that NATO pursued for decades. Against those threats, security cannot be defined in the way NATO used to define it, by counting units and weapons and by analyzing logical if complex scenarios.

Instead, the threats are ill-defined, unpredictable, and to a considerable extent even undefinable. They can also come from a wider range of sources and directions.

The Germans see new threats to their east that are in some ways more fearsome than the old. They may be inchoate and shapeless as well as imprecise, but they must be regarded as very serious:

- With the breakup of the Soviet Union, there are now several newly independent nuclear powers in the world. Two of them—Ukraine and Kazakhstan—each have more nuclear warheads on their soil than do France and Great Britain together, and even the third—Belarus—has enough such warheads to destroy Germany several times over. They do not have actual control of those weapons, which remain in the hands of the central military forces of Russia and the collapsing Commonwealth of Independent States (CIS), but the mere presence of the weapons must give Germany something to think about. Former U.S. secretary of state James Baker was able to persuade the three states to turn over their weapons to Russia by the end of the 1990s for destruction so that Soviet-American arms control accords could be implemented and expanded. In the meantime, however, the weapons remain in place.
- The risks of conflict between the new republics are very real. Several have begun to shape independent armies, and many of them have either territorial and ethnic disputes with others. The Russian populations in several of the smaller republics could generate crises between Russia and those republics. Russia and the Ukraine have a number of old quarrels, as do other states. Borders created or shifted by the central Soviet government are now being challenged by the new republics. International conflict could erupt again on the European continent after half a century of peace.
- Equally troublesome, perhaps, is the risk of power vacuums that outsiders might try to rush in to fill, either in the CIS area or in Eastern Europe. Any state that appears unable to defend itself may appear a tempting target, and it may well ask for Western help. How the West will actually handle such requests, and whether Western states will be able to handle them jointly or will begin to take sides, will do more than any other question to determine whether the Europe of the twenty-first century will be that of the nineteenth or will have evolved to a more stable form.
- The potential for devastation and mass flight arising from such conflicts or from civil wars is incalculable. The crisis in the former Yugoslavia has generated about two million refugees, and there are rumors of further potential crises in Eastern and Southeastern Europe. Those would not only create more refugees but they could draw in other countries. They might make it impossible to have the kind of economic and social progress that those countries badly need and that Germany is counting on—and supporting—for stability to its east.

- The most difficult threat in some ways is the least military in character: it is the risk of waves of refugees coming from the East not to escape war but to flee persecution, deprivation, starvation, or whatever might occur. They would be impossible to turn back, although they could perhaps be stopped near the border by vast programs of humanitarian relief. But they raise the most difficult questions, not only about the character of the countries from which they might come but also about the very soul of the countries to which they might wish to go.

Such potential developments not only raise the specter of conflict or confusion. They also raise questions about how to deter such conflict and how to deal with it. Ethnic and territorial rivalries have an emotional quality that often ignores the traditional instruments of deterrence. Western support for one or another republic against another can invite precisely the sequence of events that led to World War I. Deterrence may not work in Russia, the CIS, or Eastern Europe, but nobody is sure what will.

Nor do those scenarios constitute the only threats. Russia, a great power, remains. Even without massive forces across Eastern Europe, it compels fear by its very presence, armament, and weight. It remains a hulking menace, especially if it returns to military or ideological totalitarianism. Many Germans question whether Russia has found its definitive form of government, and there are continuing indications that the Russian military may be returning to its traditional character as a state within a state, subject theoretically to political direction but also quite able to determine what guidance it will accept and what it will reject.

A significant American presence can, therefore, be very comforting, even with a new role and as part of a new strategy. But at this point a new strategy involving American military forces and even others is only beginning to take shape. NATO has been shifting elements of its original rationale while keeping others in place. And the precise number of American forces that might be suitable for any strategy is difficult to define in the face of amorphous threats. Defining that number is as much political and psychological as military in the more limited sense.

NATO foreign ministers agreed at Copenhagen in June, 1991, that the alliance now had four main functions:

1. to provide one of the foundations for stability in Europe by making it impossible for any country to intimidate or to impose hegemony on any other by force;
2. to serve as a forum for allied consultations;
3. to deter or defend against any threat of aggression against any NATO member state; and
4. to preserve the strategic balance in Europe.

NATO has also offered places to the former enemies, although it has decided not to accept applications from those states for full NATO membership. Genscher and Baker suggested a North Atlantic Cooperation Council (NACC) to which those states could belong, and other NATO members agreed. The NACC would have no military functions and would not be in a position to instruct the Supreme Headquarters for Allied Forces in Europe (SHAPE), the operating head-quarters, but it would offer a place for common discussion of European security issues that might not properly fit into the agenda of the CSCE. The French gov-ernment opposed establishing the NACC, as it might strengthen NATO, but the German government supported it. Russia, the Baltic states, and most East European states were admitted in December, 1991, and the new republics (Belarus, Ukraine, Kazakhstan, etc.) joined in March, 1992.

The NACC has met several times in full session and has begun to carry some weight. It has voted approval of the Conventional Forces in Europe (CFE) treaty, arranging large-scale and widespread troop reductions, and has also been per-ceived as a potential instrument through which East European forces could join international peace-keeping operations. It represents an area in which Germany and the United States have been able to coordinate an important shift in the European environment.

Coupled with the earlier London Declaration of July, 1990, the new steps shift the emphasis of the North Atlantic alliance from its original deterrent role to a wider role that combines military deterrence with political reassurance. The members of the new Cooperative Council do not benefit from NATO protection as the original members of NATO did, but NATO can contribute to broad stability and security. Germany has committed itself more than any other state to such a wider concept of NATO's role, and the United States has accepted it. Washington has sent a new SHAPE commander, General John Shalikashvili, who was born in Warsaw and whose origins suggest that the Americans understand the need for a new type of American commander.

NATO's plans to deal with a potential European conflict are changing as the force levels and apparent intentions of European states are changing. The kinds of wars that might be fought in Europe will almost certainly be very different from those that were originally expected by NATO planners. NATO is abandoning the "layer cake" concept, under which NATO states have been responsible for defend-ing or helping to defend a clearly assigned stretch of the border. Instead, NATO will have highly mobile forces to fight wherever a crisis may erupt. This will force major changes in military structures, doctrines, and equipment.

NATO defense ministers have agreed to establish seven mobile corps units of still undecided size but large enough to sustain themselves in combat or in other operations. They have also agreed to establish a Rapid Reaction Force under British command that could theoretically be deployed within or outside Europe. These forces are not yet constituted, may not be constituted for some time, and will almost certainly be understaffed by cold war standards, but the very con-ception of such a force demonstrates the difference in current military thinking from the earlier.

NATO is also changing its doctrine. It has abandoned "forward defense" for "forward presence." That change reflects not only the larger space that NATO can now have for operations and maneuver but also NATO's wish to reassure its friendly Eastern neighbors that they will not become part of the battleground. NATO no longer speaks of "first use" of nuclear weapons but instead calls them weapons "of last resort." NATO also agreed in a meeting of the NPG at Taormina in October, 1991, to reduce the number of U.S. nuclear weapons in Europe by about 80 percent, removing the artillery shells and short-range missiles and keeping only the nuclear bombs. That agreement has been carried out.

The main difficulty for NATO has been to determine whether its original mission of protecting Western Europe and the North Atlantic area is still necessary and, if so, how to do it. Without the likelihood of a Soviet attack, the alliance has lost a principal purpose and an easily definable challenge. But it still has to provide contingency insurance, and it is trying to find ways to meet the new potential threats.

In June, 1992, the NATO Council decided to make it possible for NATO forces to function as peace-keepers throughout all of Europe, opening the possibility that they might become involved in the Yugoslav crisis or in the increasingly violent dispute between the former Soviet republics of Armenia and Azerbaijan over Nagorno-Karabakh. But the NATO forces can only be called in at the request of the Conference on Security and Cooperation in Europe (CSCE), which is unlikely to act because it cannot agree to concrete measures except on the basis of a unanimous vote. France objected to this additional NATO role, but the United States, Great Britain, and Germany prevailed in the Council. Nonetheless, the French can use their veto in the CSCE to block any request to NATO, effectively neutralizing any prospect that the Council's decision will actually be implemented.

NATO had earlier even ventured to undertake some undefined responsibilities throughout Central and Eastern Europe. After the Moscow coup in August, 1991, NATO issued a ministerial declaration stating that the security of the states of Central and Eastern Europe was "of direct and material concern." This in effect extended the NATO umbrella further to the east, although it did so under special circumstances and did not assert that an attack on those states was the same as an attack on NATO territory. On these as on other NATO questions, Germany and the United States have acted in agreement.

EUROPEAN AND FRANCO-GERMAN
DEFENSE PLANS

Germany and the United States have not agreed, however, and do not agree, about the development of a European force separate from NATO, and Germany has found itself caught in a bitter feud between Washington and Paris. Even at the risk of damaging German-American relations, Chancellor Kohl and his government have been tilting toward Paris.

As NATO shaped its new plans, France pressed for a separate European defense force complementary to NATO but not under NATO control. President François Mitterrand sharply criticized elements of the revised NATO architecture. He complained that the American government and others had not adequately consulted him about NATO plans, especially about such steps as the Rapid Reaction Force under British command. In retaliation, he pressed hard for German membership in a separate European force. He did so not only out of a sense of pique, however, but out of strategic considerations emerging from the traditional French role as a continental, not a maritime, power. In effect, he wanted to establish a continental force separate from that of the Atlantic states, and he may also have wanted to remove the European base of the global concert.

Such a force would theoretically be able to act in conflicts that might not be regarded as important by the Atlantic states because they would not shift the European balance of power sufficiently to affect the interests of the United States or of the other maritime states of the global concert. Those conflicts might, nonetheless, have enough impact on Europe itself to warrant some form of intervention.

Chancellor Kohl has accepted the French argument. In October, 1991, he agreed to the formation of a joint German-French Corps as the nucleus for a European force. That corps could justify the continued presence of French forces in Germany—Mitterrand announced in 1990 that he would withdraw them because of German unification—and is theoretically to be joined in the long run by other European forces. Several European states have considered joining, but they initially expressed irritation that the decision to establish the corps was made without detailed continental consultation.

France and Germany have also pledged to reinvigorate the Western European Union (WEU), originally formed in 1948 as an instrument of European collective defense. WEU headquarters is to be moved to Brussels, the seat of the European Community, in conformity with the long-term prospect that this corps would be linked to the European Community and perhaps under EC direction. Brussels is also, of course, the seat of the NATO Council.

A military command would give the EC a major new function, although its actual implementation would depend upon the final form of the Maastricht agreement. If it were to come about, and if the Maastricht agreement were to be fully ratified and carried out, Western Europe would have not only its own economy, its own currency, its own central bank, and its own parliament but also its own central political structure and its own army. It would have much of the authority and many of the trappings of a sovereign state, although they would probably be exercised under a federal rather than a centralized system. There are questions about whether all Community members would ever permit so much transfer of power to a centralized international bureaucracy, but the plans for a European army are moving ahead.

Plans for a West European force separate from NATO deeply disturbed the

U.S. government. Two Washington officials traveled to Europe in early 1991 to voice strong U.S. reservations about any independent European system. The intervention was derided as clumsy by many European and American commentators, but it achieved its effect of alerting the Europeans—and especially the Germans—to U.S. sensitivities. Later, in December 1991, President Bush voiced similar reservations when he challenged the NATO summit in Rome to decide if European defense moves would make the American commitment superfluous. He was roundly reassured that this would not happen, solving the problem for the immediate future but not ending French insistence and German concurrence that a separate European system remained necessary.

For Washington, the European Corps represents even more of a problem than a Franco-German Corps, for the latter might be only a small contingent whereas the former could be a significant force. If it were to be established, and if it were independent of NATO and SHAPE, it would confuse commanders and staff, would complicate training and logistics, and would run the risk of jeopardizing the U.S. ability to help deal with crises in Europe. It could perhaps deal with some situations in which American forces would not want to be involved, but it might also water down the entire doctrine of deterrence by leaving Western policies and resource commitments in question. French officials have left enough doubts about the emergency assignment of the Franco-German Corps (and thus of the European Corps) to reinforce American reservations.

Despite these substantive reservations, strongly voiced by U.S. officials from the president on down, the Germans have gone ahead. On May 22, 1992, at a Franco-German Defense and Security Council summit in La Rochelle, President Mitterrand and Chancellor Kohl announced definite plans for the creation of the Franco-German Corps as the first element of a European force and the initial stage of its formation. The corps is to be ready for action by October 1, 1995. The joint communiqué announcing the results of the summit stated that the European corps would contribute to strengthening the European arm of NATO, but it also made clear that the Corps would contribute to the formation of the West European Union as the defensive arm of the European union—not as an arm of NATO—and that it would also establish the basis for a European defense identity. Many U.S. officials were bitterly disappointed when the La Rochelle agreement was announced, regarding any NATO link as lip service.

The new corps is to have three missions: (1) common European defense, under NATO or the WEU; (2) peace-keeping and peace-making; and (3) humanitarian missions.

The corps will not operate under the geographic limitations of the NATO treaty and can theoretically thus function in areas where German troops have not gone since World War II. This might be one of the points that would make it attractive to Bonn and Paris.

The German forces in the corps can now be assigned to only two of the three corps missions, the defense of Europe and humanitarian tasks. As indicated in

Chapter 8, German peace-keeping, and especially peace-making, missions re-main controversial in Germany itself and might even be questioned by some of Germany's allies. The German government is considering an amendment to the German Basic Law in order to permit German forces to undertake such missions outside the traditional NATO area. Some Europeans believe that German public opinion might be more likely to permit such missions under a European rather than under a NATO command, and certainly more ready to undertake them under a multinational rather than under a national flag.

Whether that is true or not, the German forces of a Franco-German or a European Corps would be under much greater pressure to join in international operations than they would be under NATO, for NATO has more members and it is easier for individual states to decline particular missions. The Franco-German Corps, therefore, could well hasten the day when German forces will again oper-ate outside the NATO area.

The relations to be established between the new corps and NATO remain ambiguous. Even before the Franco-German summit, at the EC summit at Maastricht in December of 1991, there was talk of an "emerging European securi-ty and defense identity." It was also envisaged that the WEU states would coordi-nate their views in order to have a joint position in NATO meetings. There was also, however, the assertion that the Atlantic alliance was to remain the essential forum for consultation for defense matters. These ambiguities leave enough room for interpretation to place the Germans repeatedly in a position where they have to choose between two principal allies as well as between a European and an Atlantic vocation.

In December, 1992, it was announced that Germany and France would be prepared to have the Franco-German Corps (and, by extension, the Euro-Corps) assigned to NATO command in an emergency, but only if its integrity was respected. This would give NATO nominal command of the European force but has the dis-advantage that once the Euro-Corps becomes a major force it might be difficult for NATO to assign it as a unit and thus difficult to incorporate it into NATO plans.

German officers have told Americans that the French government, and espe-cially President Mitterrand, want no reference to NATO in documents referring to the new Franco-German Corps and that he agreed to include the phrases about the WEU-NATO link only after the German government and the chancellor had insisted upon them. The Germans believe, therefore, that they have succeeded in shifting the French position toward NATO.

After the Franco-German summit in May 1992 that announced the Franco-German Corps, Chancellor Kohl went so far as to write a personal letter assuring President Bush of Germany's continuing loyalty to NATO.

The French government has argued that a European force is necessary because the United States will not remain in Europe but will eventually withdraw, and that Europe needs to prepare its own force before that withdrawal. It has also argued that the anti-Soviet commitment which the United States originally made in NATO is neither credible nor pertinent to the new types of threats on the horizon.

Whether or not these assertions might be true, it is certainly true that the Americans are much more likely to withdraw if they believe that they are not wanted or needed. Moves toward a separate European force have reinforced the convictions and the arguments of congressional proponents of an early U.S. withdrawal from Europe. The German government, therefore, faces the risk of creating a self-fulfilling prophecy that might redound adversely to German interests as perceived in Washington, and that would also redound adversely to U.S. interests.

The Yugoslav crisis again underlined the differences in American and French perceptions. When the United Nations authorized the establishment and enforcement of a "no-fly" zone above certain parts of Bosnia to help protect civilians from air attacks, the United States wanted to use the NATO structure to direct Western operations because NATO was well organized and had command over the necessary operational and logistical assets. France agreed to operate under NATO, but only if it was made clear that NATO was acting under a U.N. banner. Although this measure could be interpreted more as a face-saving device than a practical one, it again illustrated the difficulties of finding a solution that would please all parties that might need to operate side by side in a future Europe.

There are also many doubts in the minds of American observers whether this Franco-German idea is truly supported in Western Europe as a whole. The Council of Ministers of the West European Union did not even mention the European Corps or the Franco-German Corps in its Petersburg Declaration of June 23, 1992, and a number of European officers have told Americans that they would rather continue to cooperate with U.S. forces in NATO than with a separate Franco-German force. The smaller European continental states worry about German or Franco-German dominance unrestrained by a U.S. presence. The specter of future German dominance, now restrained by the U.S. presence, is apparently one of the reservations felt by other Europeans.

FUTURE U.S. FORCE LEVELS

There are already countless pressures in the United States to reduce U.S. forces in Europe. One full corps, the U.S. VII Corps, has been withdrawn from Germany. Many U.S. bases have already been closed, and more are scheduled to be closed by 1995.

The U.S. Department of Defense has proposed a gradual reduction of forces to 150,000 by 1996. That level would leave a U.S. corps of 70,000 personnel with full air, naval, and logistic support. Pentagon planning documents published at the end of May, 1992, envisage close U.S. cooperation with American allies to maintain a system of international defense coordination. With U.S. defense expenditures as a percentage of American gross domestic product at their lowest levels since the 1970s, American cooperation with allies becomes essential in order to preserve a global structure of military security for the United States and for those allies.

The U.S. Congress, however, is pushing for a much more accelerated schedule of withdrawals from Europe and from other U.S. global outposts. Senator Sam

Nunn and (then) Representative Les Aspin, two powerful congressional leaders who concentrate on defense matters, said in 1992 that U.S. forces in Europe should be reduced over time to well below 150,000—perhaps to 75,000. Other members of Congress such as Representative Pat Schroeder have called for votes to lower the ceiling immediately to 100,000 with further cuts to follow, and the House of Representatives has passed a defense budget requiring accelerated reductions in U.S. forces assigned to Europe and far fewer than 100,000 U.S. military in Germany by 1995. With Aspin having become secretary of defense for President Clinton in 1993, he will be in a position to implement a withdrawal of American forces.

The governing factor is the American budget process, which is difficult to predict and which is increasingly oriented toward domestic instead of foreign concerns. Since the end of the cold war, as indicated in Chapter 5, the U.S. defense budget has been under pressure. The only widely accepted justification for defense expenditures is now the employment that they can provide in the United States. In the budget for fiscal year 1994, which will be debated by the U.S. Congress during 1993, it will be possible to transfer funds from the military budget to domestic programs. Members of Congress will want to reduce the defense budget to spend the funds on domestic purposes. They will also want to make certain that even the military funds that remain will be spent at home rather than abroad. These pressures will combine to accelerate the reduction of U.S. forces in Germany, but not necessarily to eliminate them.

With the end of the cold war, it is more difficult to justify a large U.S. force in Europe. Several arguments have been proposed, but they have not so far generated the kind of widespread American popular and political support that the earlier U.S. mission commanded:

- One argument is that U.S. forces offer a form of reassurance to Germany and to other states—in Eastern as well as Western Europe—that there is an American presence on the continent to balance a potentially resurgent Russia.
- Another is that most of the small and perhaps even some of the larger European states will see an American presence as a balancing factor against overwhelming German power.
- A third argument is that the U.S. forces in Europe reflect the U.S. interest in the continent, and that this interest remains even after the end of the cold war.
- Fourth, and perhaps most important to the United States itself, American forces in Europe can help implement U.S. global responsibilities implied by President Bush's announced concept of the new world order. This argument recalls German-American cooperation in deploying U.S. forces and equipment from Germany to the Gulf, but many elements of German opinion oppose the suggestion that Germany would provide a large aircraft carrier

on which the United States could base forces designed and intended to operate outside Europe—perhaps in areas where Germany might not have identical interests with the United States.

The conditions under which U.S. forces can remain could become another important element in the American decision on force levels in Europe. In the post–cold war Status of Forces negotiations that began in 1991 and were concluded at the end of 1992, the German negotiators have insisted that certain American training habits such as nighttime training or low flying be curtailed so as not to disturb the German population (which, some polls suggest, is not as friendly to the presence of American soldiers as before). They also want to limit the size and range of military maneuvers. But the U.S. military, always conscious of its obligation to go anywhere at any time under potential battle conditions, will regard those restrictions as onerous. So might individual officers and career soldiers who need that training to maintain their career status.

Germany, like the United States, has held a debate about force levels. As of this writing there is no official indication that the German force level might sink below the 370,000 limit which was agreed to by the Soviet Union when Germany was united (along with the CSCE ceiling of 345,000 for ground and air forces). Members of the German government have said that they would not want to go below that level, and it appears unlikely that force levels would sink quickly as long as large numbers of Soviet forces remain in Eastern Germany. Over the long run, however, if Europe remains militarily stable, the number of German forces will almost certainly be reduced below 300,000 and perhaps below 250,000 as a means of reassurance to Western European as well as other states. One German corps has already been withdrawn from NATO.

The new military situation presents a paradox for German-American relations. On the one hand, if the two countries stand down from their common defense alert, that will reduce if not end the periodic German-American debates about strategy and tactics. On the other, such an action removes a powerful element of German-American cooperation. Germans and Americans have been comrades in arms, even if they have periodically disagreed. They could often overcome other problems because they both knew that they needed each other for protection. That knowledge was, at least to some extent, the glue that held them together. It provided a firm basis for wider mutual cooperation.

FRANCE, GERMANY, AND
THE GLOBAL CONCERT

France, like historical Germany, has long believed that the maritime powers of the global concert were not its true friends. Although France has been at peace with England during the twentieth century and has been allied to England and the United States during the two world wars and the cold war, any French official can cite many instances when the maritime powers did not pay sufficient attention to French interests either during the world wars, between them, or since. The French government believes that France has not had, and does not have, identical interests with those of the maritime powers, and that those maritime powers all too often go their own way. The French phrase "les Anglo-Saxons," usually used in a derisory sense, reflects this French conviction.

Even during the cold war, the French government often distanced itself visibly and deliberately from American and British policies, either in Europe—where it withdrew from the NATO integrated command—or elsewhere.

France, like Germany, has been primarily a continental power, although it has historically played a much more global role than Germany. Unlike Britain and the United States, France was vulnerable to continental enemies and had to concentrate on continental diplomacy, continental politics, and continental strategy.

Like Germany, France now wants to shape the new Europe, especially as the Soviet collapse has again made Europe an important arena for international politics and strategy. President Mitterrand may have wanted to delay and perhaps even prevent the reunification of Germany in the period immediately after the breach of the Berlin Wall, but he later supported unification in order to win the friendship of a united Germany. France has recognized that it cannot conduct a European strategy without German support.

France also has long resisted and resented American dominance of the global concert. The United States never supported the French colonial system, failing to support France in Indochina in 1954 and in North Africa later. It has rarely shared French views about the Middle East and Africa, opposing the French intervention at Suez in 1956 and often differing from French policy thereafter. President Mitterrand was said to have reacted with genuine anger that Great Britain was given command of the NATO Rapid Reaction Force, and he certainly does not want the United States or Britain to be able to veto European military operations within or outside Europe. With the collapse of the Soviet imperium, France sees a new situation, one in which Europe for the first time in fifty years no longer needs the United States and in which Europe can act on its own.

France was never to become the cold war bastion of the global concert in Europe that West Germany was to become. Its independent attitudes and policies always made it a separate European actor, especially after the return of Charles de Gaulle to power in 1958. Its determination to support and advance the European Community, other European organizations, and separate European scientific, industrial, and intellectual development has given it a core role in Europe. The military element now being added through the Franco-German Corps and the prospective European Corps will establish a potentially separate European strategic structure, not only for defense but also for operations outside Western Europe and the continent as a whole.

Germany must have a different perspective on this. Germany's military security and political freedom were based for forty-five years on its association with the United States, with American nuclear weapons, and with the global reach of U.S. power. Germany also provided a base for the further projection of that power. It was a core member of the global concert, even though it was deep within Europe, and its association with that concert was much more thorough and intimate than that of France.

The association with the maritime powers, and especially with the United States, provided Germany with a more stable security base than any past arrangement had provided. The link with America gave Germany safety without threatening or appearing to threaten others. Germany did not have to provide for its own security through either conquering or dominating other continental states, or through an alliance system that might have intimidated those who were not in it. Germany could be safe without making others feel unsafe. It was secure without making others insecure.

France, of course, had its own nuclear force, a separate military identity, and a protective cordon manned by three-quarters of a million NATO troops in West Germany and elsewhere. It could therefore conduct a more independent policy than could Germany, although it always took care to make certain that it and the NATO command were informed about each other's strategic plans. Even now, it remains protected by German territory from the last remaining potential European continental great power, Russia, and from many of the new threats arising in Eastern Europe and beyond.

U.S. officials who question the German move are warning that military alliances require more demanding coordination than any other types of associations. Diplomatic and political coordination can be done by telephone calls, some cabled instructions, and perhaps a quick conference. Economic coordination can be done by phone calls as well, whether between finance ministers or central bankers, and the mechanisms for coordinated market interventions are so well established that they can be triggered immediately. Military coordination, however, requires detailed planning, mutually agreed upon force levels, types, armament, equipment, and missions, coordinated logistics and very precisely understood command and control arrangements. It cannot be done overnight but takes weeks and sometimes months or even years of coordinated training and maneuvers. Therefore, on the military side, any damage to established structures will be more difficult and more tedious to repair, and the Euro-Corps will sooner or later not be able to function with NATO no matter what may now be said or planned unless there is very intimate coordination even when there is no emergency in view.

German officials dispute this conclusion. They argue that the Franco-German Corps and the European Corps will actually draw France closer to the NATO alliance through the German connection. They point out that they have repeatedly made certain that European documents like the Maastricht declaration link the WEU and NATO. They describe the Franco-German Corps as a building block toward a European political union, as part of "making Europe" but not as part of splitting Europe off from the Atlantic powers. French officials insist that it is not so. They state categorically that France retains as much independence from NATO as ever, no matter what NATO and European declarations may claim and no matter what the Germans may say.

The German government may actually, however, be quietly reflecting a new strategic reality, which is that it now really prefers a different type of alliance system. The NATO system, partly because of the American experience at Pearl Harbor and the fear of Soviet surprise attack, was always geared to a rapid and well-prepared response based on prepositioned forces and long-established contingency plans. German military and defense officials have never fully shared the particular American affinity for such plans (the German High Command in World War I did not even execute its own Schlieffen Plan).

A European force, less tightly structured and more flexible in its planning, equipment, training, and operational concepts, might not only be more appropriate to the new situation in Europe but might correspond more closely to German desires for flexibly structured and calibrated responses. As this force probably would not need the transatlantic defense-in-depth backing that was essential to defend Germany against a nuclear superpower, it could perhaps dispense with the U.S. guarantee and with the American operating style.

Like France, Germany might also want to act in situations where the United States might not be prepared to act, and Germany would not want to be tied to Washington's views on where or where not to intervene. A great deal would depend, of course, on whether German forces receive Basic Law clearance for operations outside the NATO area.

In the new situation, trying to establish a continental defense, Germany may need France more than it needs America. The Paris-Bonn (and later Paris-Berlin) connection provides a political and strategic core for Europe itself. Without it, there can be no European security identity—or at least no such identity separate from NATO. Such a Franco-German army can perhaps not afford to maintain the kind of advanced research facilities that the United States maintains. Therefore, it will not be—and will almost certainly not remain—at the front line of global military technology (as the Gulf War demonstrated). But the German and French governments might believe that their military technology will be adequate for the missions that a European force is likely to perform.

One point is clear, however: The German decision to take part in a separate or separable European defense structure has consequences that go well beyond the Franco-German or even the European Corps. This decision goes to the heart of the future organization of the European continent and to the heart of the American role in Europe and even to the heart of the American power position in the world. If the German decision has the effect of pulling Germany gradually out of NATO, the Germans themselves will have achieved what the Soviet Union consistently tried and failed to achieve during the cold war and the Two-plus-Four negotiations. They will thus have undercut the great success of Chancellor Kohl and President Bush in those negotiations. They may believe that a NATO connection is no longer necessary.

More worrisome, however, is whether the removal of the Franco-German forces from NATO, matching the pullback of the European Community from GATT, might begin to constitute a true withdrawal of the European continental system across the board from the global concert. If that turns out to be correct, and if that is the intent of French or even of German policy, it would be a decision of far-reaching, even historic, importance.

It is little wonder that the American government tried hard to persuade the German government to desist. And nothing baffles American friends of Germany more than the feeling that Germany is deliberately abandoning and even perhaps destroying a system that has worked, and that they believe has defended German interests. They cannot understand how the German government can believe, or at least claim that it believes, that its decision changes nothing.

It is not the future of the European military system that is at stake, but the political control of Europe and the structure of the global system. The American government would like to retain as much influence as possible, keeping Germany in the global concert and Europe in the global system. This would have immense advantages for the Germans because American power can continue to give Germany security without arousing fears of German dominance in Western or Eastern Europe. But Germany may not want this kind of arrangement any longer. Germany may be losing confidence in the United States. The intense American congressional and public debate about the future American world role, and the many voices calling for drastic U.S. force reductions around the world, may convince senior German officials that America is no longer a reliable partner.

French officials tell Americans privately that senior Germans agree with the French assessment that the United States will not retain a European presence, but that the Germans have long ago lost their ability to talk frankly to the Americans and are now constrained from saying what they believe. If that is so, then Germany must indeed leave the American system and choose a continental one.

The end of the cold war returned to Germany not only its unity but also its power of decision and thus its strategic responsibility. The Germans are now free to decide their own strategy more freely than before, and also to select those who are to be their closest associates. The French position forces Germany to choose quickly, perhaps before it is fully ready, and the German choices that are being made every day will help to change the shape of Europe.

If Germany joins France in a separate European force, Germany will in effect begin to withdraw from the global concert. It will also weaken that global concert. American forces will be less likely to find a welcome in Germany. They will also be precluded from using German bases as freely as before for operations beyond Europe. A German decision to assign troops to a European force is a much more profound break with postwar history than is a French decision, and its effects will be serious for Germany, for Europe, for the United States, and for the global system. It could affect German relations with Great Britain as well as with the United States. This decision means that Germany is opening the door to its return to a continental function, and it will ultimately remove the European continent from the global security system.

With America itself pulling back, and with Germany turning elsewhere, the strategic arch that the two states established across the Atlantic is losing the pedestals on which it rested at both ends, and each government is reinforcing and confirming the other's fears.

It is, therefore, in the area of military cooperation that the sharpest departure has come since 1990 from the pattern of earlier German-American relations.

Defense is also, however, an area in which the two states may actually need to cooperate more closely in future. For Western Europe and Germany cannot be wholly secure as long as Russia and Eastern Europe are in real or potential turmoil. The risk of conflict remains. And the United States is not fully secure if Europe is in danger. Moreover, Germany needs a strong nuclear partner, prepared to protect German interests in a crisis, in order to avoid having a rancorous domestic debate about whether or not Germany should have its own nuclear weapons.

The United States cannot be truly secure if its only allies are maritime powers. Germany cannot be truly secure if its only allies are continental powers. In a broad sense, therefore, they can both continue to benefit from a mutual defense association.

For these reasons, Germany and the United States should conduct close defense consultations, within the NATO context, in order to determine what structures can best suit their common needs. They should also use those consultations to agree on the best role and size for American forces, if for no other reason than to make certain that U.S. force levels are not decided solely on the basis of passing political arguments in both countries.

In military affairs, the two states had their most intimate if sometimes contentious collaboration during the cold war. After German unification it has become the area in which they may first choose to look for new and separate paths. Yet it is also an area in which they still have many common interests and in which they still need each other, even if not exactly in the same way as in the past.

Part Three
THE GERMANY
THAT CAN SAY NO

11

THE RIFT IN
THE GLOBAL CONCERT

The first part of this book showed that with the cold war over, Germany and the United States now face radically new situations at home, in Europe, and in the world. It showed that the foundations for their relationship have shifted profoundly, and that they both face new and difficult responsibilities.

The crucial new responsibility that Germany now faces is to help design the new post–cold war order. Such a task is unprecedented for Germany, which has been more accustomed to losing than winning wars in the twentieth century. A second, equally important, responsibility is to keep the new united Europe and the maritime democracies together within the global concert while also changing the global concert itself. And Germany has to accomplish these tasks while dealing with the increasingly complicated and costly problems generated by its own unification.

The crucial responsibility that the United States now faces is to hold together the alliance that won the cold war victory and to use that alliance to shape a new order. Such a task is unprecedented for America, which has seen two of its alliance systems (after World Wars I and II) collapse during this century after their purposes had been achieved. Washington must also find this new foreign policy at a time when many Americans want only to reduce their obligations abroad.

The second part of the book showed that the two states are reacting to the new situation by moving apart, not by staying together, and that they are following increasingly divergent courses in political, economic, and military matters. It also showed that they are not adjusting their policies to each other's needs.

If the first years after German unification are a sign of what is to come, German-American cooperation will not last to the year 2000 and perhaps not even until 1995. And the world coalition, which Germany and the United States anchored for decades, will not last any longer.

This divergence came about at a time when the leaders in Bonn and Washington claimed to be personally committed to German-American collaboration. The change to a new German generation that has not had the postwar experience of cooperation, a prospect that has long worried many Germans and Americans, has not even arrived yet. Nor has the equally feared and equally often predicted shift

107

toward a more isolationist government in the United States. President Clinton shows no sign of wanting to return to isolationism, although he wants to concentrate more of his attention on domestic priorities.

President George Bush and Chancellor Helmut Kohl were good personal friends and were committed to close cooperation. Bush helped Kohl get reelected in 1990, and Kohl expressed his support for Bush's reelection in 1992. Kohl has also made immense contributions to the advancement of German-American studies in the United States. Yet the two men were moving in separate directions during much of 1991 and 1992. By the time Bush left office, he and Kohl had little left to say to each other. They did not even bother to have a farewell meeting, although they could have easily arranged to have one as Bush was on his way back from Moscow in the last weeks of his presidency.

The new German foreign minister, Klaus Kinkel, is a friend of the United States. He has had excellent relations with American officials for almost two decades, since the time when he was chief of the Foreign Office Planning Staff. But even he, in his initial policy statements, showed no signs that he would or could change basic German policy. He did, however, ease German-American political tensions over the Balkans, and he has persistently offered better or at least clearer explanations to the worried American government.

The new American secretary of state, Warren Christopher, has made an effort to show that he can have good relations with Germany. He worked closely with Germans while he was deputy secretary of state for President Jimmy Carter during the late 1970s. He then got help from Foreign Minister Hans-Dietrich Genscher in trying to gain the release of Americans held hostage in Iran, an effort for which Genscher periodically served as an intermediary.

The new U.S. president, Bill Clinton, is also a friend of Germany. As indicated earlier, he used to visit Germany when he was a student at Oxford University. He has expressed admiration for some German management techniques, such as vocational training. He has encouraged his daughter, Chelsea, to learn German, and they are said to converse occasionally in German.

But these friendships and common personal interests cannot have real meaning when there are divergences of national interests or of perceptions of national interests. And those divergences do now exist. More important, perhaps, the many common interests appear less important.

The days when German and American soldiers stood side by side on the border between the East and the West, or when the U.S. Army was guaranteeing the freedom of West Berlin, may not have disappeared from memory, but they have certainly vanished from daily policy consideration. In their place are countless debates and arguments, sometimes public and sometimes private, between Bonn and Washington.

The United States and Germany have not always agreed in the past. They have argued about many things, including policy toward the former Soviet Union, military strategy, and global monetary policies. But what has changed is the quality of the relationship. Earlier, disagreements appeared to be exceptions, not habits. Now, they threaten to become habits. Earlier, both countries knew that they would ultimately have to agree, and they talked to each other with that expectation in mind. Now, they no longer appear to believe that they do have to agree. Yet the global concert, the worldwide structure that they helped to build and to protect, remains as essential to both of them as it was during the cold war.

It may be that the changes in the world came so fast that neither country has yet had time to adjust. Attitudes often change more slowly than realities. Perhaps Bonn and Washington will recover a sense of common purpose in the light of the many common interests that remain. But divergence has become a habit rather than an exception, and it is the kind of habit that feeds on itself as countries begin to look elsewhere rather than to each other for support.

THE TWO GERMAN QUESTIONS
AND THE TWO AMERICAN QUESTIONS

For the United States, as for the Germans and for others, there have long been two German questions:

The first German question always arose when Germany was divided and weak, as it was throughout most of modern European history. Then, the question was who would fight over the pieces of Germany that were lying on the international chessboard, who might dominate Germany, and who might use one group of Germans either against other Germans or against other states. This was the question that agitated French emperor Napoleon, Austrian chancellor Metternich, and countless other statesmen, and it also kept the United States and the global concert in the center of Europe from 1945 to 1990.

The second question always arose when Germany was united and potentially or actually powerful, as from 1871 through 1945. Then, the nations of Europe and elsewhere worried about what the German people and the German state would do to them and to the global order. This is the question that is now being posed again, although in a different form than in the past, and that nobody can answer. Many fear a united Germany, even when it is democratic and peace-loving. They know that Germany can make decisions that will shape Europe and much of the world, and they fear that it will make those decisions on the basis of its own interests rather than on the basis of the interests of others.

Much of the history of the past two centuries can be written in terms of the German question, or of the two German questions. It remains to be seen whether the second, the basic, question can be answered in the next century, by Germans and by others.

German leaders know that they now must try to answer that second German question. It is one of the burdens of unity, and perhaps the most difficult one. They must answer it not only for the Americans, who are far away, but for the many smaller and nearer European nations.

Germany now also faces two American questions, both of which had in the past plagued England and other U.S. allies more than Bonn:

First, what role will the United States play in the world now that it has won this century's third great victory? Will it pull back, as it did after the first victory, or remain engaged, as it did after the second? Specifically, will America withdraw from Europe? If it remains, will it remain only on its own terms or on the terms outlined or at least agreed by the Europeans? Will America accept a competitor who still wants to remain a friend? Will America also accept more co-direction than it has in the global system and in all the many institutions it has created to its own benefit and that of others? Will America develop a new grand strategy for the new world, and who will be invited to help plan that strategy?

Second, who speaks for America? Is it a president who cannot always achieve what he wants, an establishment that has lost its sense of direction, a Congress anxious to spend money only where it will win votes, or a business community that wants an open world but also wants government support whenever possible? What kind of president will Clinton be, a Woodrow Wilson who could not defeat the isolationists, a Harry Truman who could and did, or a new type?

Now, more than ever, the German and the American questions are intermingled, and the answers to some questions may help determine the answers to others. An America that fears or mistrusts the newly powerful Germany will decide its role in Europe on that basis. A Germany that mistrusts America's readiness to keep its commitments will behave differently from one that expects America to remain in Europe. And each answer will generate a process leading to other answers until they create a spiral whose direction and length nobody can predict. This is what is now happening.

A SPLIT IN THE GLOBAL CONCERT?

As this process advances, could the global concert itself split, with Germany and the United States leading the continental and the maritime powers in different directions? Such a split would be even more important, and potentially even more historically significant, than a split between Bonn and Washington alone or, as suggested in Chapter 10, than a split between NATO and the WEU. A global and German-American split may reinforce each other, and German-American differences may even help create a global split.

The global system and German-American ties are closely linked. German-American relations after World War II represented more than the bilateral ties between two countries and two peoples. They also helped to make Western Europe part of the global concert, giving the maritime powers a firm position on the European continent and giving West Germany and Western Europe the protection of the maritime powers. German-American relations were, and they remain, at the very core of the American position in continental Europe. The

German-American link is the fundamental foundation of the global concert's position in Europe.

The shocks to bilateral German-American relations since German unification have also affected European-American links, and they may also in some cases have reflected European-American differences.

German-American differences do not, therefore, only run the risk of destroying or damaging a connection between two states. They can also break the link between the maritime powers and continental Europe, offering the prospect of a European concert that functions on its own and that takes its own coordinated positions in the G-7, the GATT, and the global system as a whole. Is that now possible, and is it perhaps even likely?

It is certainly possible, and it may even be tempting. Europe is regaining its identity and influence, and it is safe from the long-feared Soviet threat. Germany lies astride the middle of the continent. Berlin has returned to a central position. Germany may no longer need to be the global outpost on the continent but may instead want to be at the center of its own continental concert.

The global concert was based on three elements: (1) the strategic necessity of cooperating against the Soviet and Communist threat; (2) the need for a global economic (commercial and monetary) system; and (3) the shared political ideals of the major powers.

Strategic cooperation may no longer be necessary, a global economic system may appear to be a burden rather than an opportunity, and political ideals can be shared without agreement on other matters. Therefore, the foundations for the global concert are not as strong as before, and may even be gone.

If German money can help establish the kind of Eastern Europe that is truly prosperous, and if German strategy can create a truly secure Western Europe, the German dream of sitting in the middle of a stable continent can be fulfilled. This may look more attractive than sitting in the global concert next to the United States.

Such a united Europe is, however, no simple task for Germany, but a potentially immense burden. No German leader can look at the continent without a deep frown. All the reserves and resources accumulated by West Germany during forty years cannot soon close the gap between the East and the West in Europe. All the power of German and West European arms, and all the talents of European diplomacy, cannot suppress the crises and conflicts that loom in the East.

Germany has since 1990 concentrated on its own continent (as well as on itself). It has had to do so. It cannot afford to have Europe again divided, and it cannot afford to have Europe again collapse into the kind of civil war that destroyed it during the twentieth century.

America sometimes seems far away, perhaps unconcerned or impotent, and far less relevant than it was when there was a Soviet threat. One can perhaps call on it for help, but not for the management of the continent as a whole. The worse the crises in Europe, East or West, the more Germany may be drawn away from America and from the global system.

For their part, the United States and the other non-European members of the G-7 and the global concert do not need all of Europe for their own security as they needed Western Europe against Moscow. The maritime states' political and strategic interests in Europe have always been limited, and they will remain so. Economic and commercial interests may go deeper, but those can perhaps be protected without a military presence.

The global concert under the leadership of the United States was prepared to commit itself to the freedom of Western Europe and of West Germany, and to the unity of all of Germany, but it is not prepared to link itself politically or militarily to all of Europe. Such a link would constitute a major reversal of policy as well as a profound shift in global priorities.

Thus, the United States will not try to solve all European problems, or even to play the leading role in solving them, although it might be prepared to help European states solve them if necessary. No American government can reach deeply into Eastern Europe. The American government, including the president and the Congress, will not make the same effort in continental Europe that Germany is making. Nor will Japan, Canada, or even Great Britain.

With its original task accomplished, America is beginning to reduce its presence in Europe. But it is still prepared to play a supportive role if there is a renewed threat to Western Europe from a revival of Russian imperialist ambitions or from civil wars spilling over from the East. That is one reason it wants to maintain a base structure in Western Europe. Even maritime powers—and air powers—need land bases. And any reduction in responsibilities also means a reduction in power and influence.

Even as U.S. forces are withdrawing, the American government wants Europe to remain part of the global system and of the global concert, and it especially wants Germany in that system and that concert. Washington does not want to see a split down the middle of the Atlantic Ocean or the middle of the English Channel. It also wants to be able to keep Europe as one of the chain of continents that link American power across the Northern Hemisphere and that give U.S. forces their global reach.

This lies at the core of American concerns about the future of GATT, NATO, and the G-7 as well as other institutions. A European withdrawal from GATT can lead to the end of the global system and to a fracture in the global concert. A European alternative to NATO can make it impossible for the United States to help preserve its interests in the safety of Western Europe and in keeping a European base for other operations.

Germany, and a presence in Germany, are thus essential for certain U.S. interests if not for others. Those U.S. interests may be different from Germany's, but they are still there. Nonetheless, the priorities that American strategy has in Europe often seem irrelevant to Germans and to the German government, for anything that happens in Europe can affect Germany even if it does not affect the United States.

The U.S. government would like to reduce its presence in Europe but does not want that reduction to create a Europe opposed to U.S. interests and concerns. The American government needs to devise a formula by which it can pull back from Europe without having Europe turn against the United States and without losing its influence on the continent.

Washington has clearly been counting on Bonn to make this possible by continuing to serve as America's closest ally in Europe even as the United States reduces its own presence. But recent indications are that Bonn may not be prepared to cooperate.

President François Mitterrand of France has been offering Germany an alternative to the United States and to U.S. leadership of the global concert. In effect, Mitterrand has said that France will be prepared to develop European and even Franco-German structures that can protect all German interests, not only those that coincide with U.S. interests. Mitterrand, like other French leaders before him such as former president Charles de Gaulle, believes that Europe can be better organized without the United States or at least with a much less prominent (they might say dominant) American role.

France, the traditional continental power, is offering Germany a place within a revived and revised continental system. This is not only a proposal about a new European force that will give certain German forces a priority obligation above their earlier NATO commitment. Nor is it a proposal to establish a new economic empire that will stretch from Calais to Vladivostok or at least to the Urals. It is a proposal for a new pan-European confederation based upon the European Community, French nuclear power, German economic power, and the allegiance of those who see their future in Europe rather than in the world. It binds Germany to France in ways that prevent total German domination of the European continent once history puts an end to what the French regard as American domination. Under that plan, Germany might have the eminent power role, but France would have the eminent policy role.

To underline his readiness to establish such a structure, Mitterrand has paid the price of a brutal recession that would keep France in the European Monetary System and the Exchange Rate Mechanism. He also decided to keep French forces in Germany under the Euro-Corps arrangement, although he had first stated that he would withdraw those forces. These two Franco-German links form the basic elements of a European continental system that can be independent of the United States and that does not need to fear arbitrary American decisions.

Not only Europe is at stake, however, but the shape of the world. Arguments about the relationship between NATO and the Franco-German Corps or about the Common Agricultural Policy are essentially arguments about the link between the global concert and the continental system. They are not only arguments about strategy, trade, or economics, although they have strategic, commercial, and economic effects. They are arguments about the future organization of

Europe and of the world, and about the future role of the United States in Europe.

In the French vision, a European continental system can certainly offer a place to the United States once the system is established. But it will be a place where U.S. interests will be defined by the Europeans and where the United States will not be a power factor on the continent but an invited guest. And the French, as leaders of the new Concert of Europe, will determine what the American role is to be and what the relationship is to be between the new Europe and the global system. The Germans may have a voice, however, and this may be enough for Bonn.

Several West European states have objected to the new Franco-German arrangement. They have expressed reservations about the Euro-Corps, not only because it was bilaterally established without their agreement but because they fear that it could ultimately take them out of NATO and place them under Franco-German direction. Even if they do not always agree with Washington, they want an American presence to counteract the power of Germany and to help preserve the European balance if it is indeed ever again threatened from the east. They also fear that the collapse of GATT will force them to negotiate their own trade arrangements, which they will not be able to do advantageously because they are too small and which they do not want to do only through the European Community. It is worth noting that it is the European maritime states that have objected most to the continental leanings of France and Germany.

The U.S. government in turn is upset with the German government because no French desire for a separate Europe could even be conceivable without German power and German support. If Germany decided that the time had come for a GATT accord, France would have to agree. If Germany refused to join the Franco-German Corps or even the Euro-Corps, those organizations could never be created or even imagined. The Americans believe that Bonn's policy will create precisely the result that the German government claims to fear—a substantial and perhaps complete U.S. withdrawal from the continent, and with that a split of the global concert and the global system. And Washington thinks that Germany will have created the split by making it possible.

In American eyes, Bonn is helping to create a Europe that is not only independent of the United States but working against U.S. interests. This is not what Washington wanted. Nor do the Americans believe that it is in the best interests of Germany. The Americans believe there must be a middle course between a massive U.S. presence on the continent and a total loss of U.S. influence. They want a Europe that remains in the global system even without the full-scale presence of American forces on the continent.

Chancellor Kohl and his new foreign minister, Klaus Kinkel, confront the most cruel dilemmas, because there are many reasons for Germany to let itself be drawn into a continental system:

- In the long course of European history, Franco-German hostility has been at the root of more conflicts than has any other single factor. No German statesman can miss the opportunity to end that hostility, and no German statesman would want it written that he broke the link to France.
- In the strategic realm, Germany's place is in Europe, and most of its interests can best be fulfilled there. A German government cannot be confident that the United States will now really remain in Europe, with the U.S. Congress making decisions about the U.S. military budget primarily for domestic social reasons instead of for global strategic reasons. This leaves Germany and others uncertain whether the United States will continue to fulfill its commitments.
- The new Europe needs Germany if it is to succeed. German power and money are essential. So are German influence and direction, if they can be unobtrusively and inoffensively exercised. Despite the long history of conflict and contention, European nations are prepared to work with Germany, and many in Eastern Europe want German investment and German trade. If Germany does not act, Europe may fail. European integration may stop in the West, and the new democracies may collapse in the East. Chancellor Kohl himself has warned that Europe had to be established now if at all, and Germany is central to the stability and prosperity of that Europe.
- Germany also needs Europe. Germany has always been primarily a European power, and it needs a stable situation in Europe if it is to have peace and prosperity at home. Germans want to concentrate their resources where those resources do the most good, in Europe East and West. Germany may even need to postpone a more liberal global trading system, not because of French objections but because Germany itself suddenly has open borders with what is really part of the developing world and may need to seal those borders to preserve the standard of living of the German people. Bonn may also want a sheltered European market to protect its own high-cost industries and also to be free to select its imports from Eastern Europe rather than from America or Asia. The German government can argue that even the United States is leaning more and more toward managed trade and cannot be counted on to preserve the GATT system. There is even evidence to support such a contention.
- Germany cannot afford to be seen as the agent of American strategic or economic policy when the Americans themselves are going through what may become a systemic crisis.
- French support is essential if German ideas about the future organization of Europe are to prevail. France will play the main role in deciding European Community policy and will also play a key role in deciding on the location of the new European central bank. Many Europeans will accept French ideas more readily than German ideas.

- France also has global political and commercial presence and influence. If such subsidized European and German products as the Airbus passenger jet are to sell in Asia or Africa, French support may be necessary to help sell them.

Nonetheless, the global system and the American connection still have a great deal to offer, and the global concert remains powerful and useful:

- Strategically, only the American guarantee may be strong enough to not only win a conflict but deter it. For only America, whatever its weaknesses, remains a true superpower that can not only fight but overwhelm its opponents with mass, technology, and pure resources and that can remain at the increasingly costly forefront of military technology. It has the only military forces in the world that can truly deter a potential Russian lurch into Bonapartism.
- Economically, Europe as a sole economic arena for its countries is confining even if it is comfortable. Over the long run, as German and other economists have pointed out, Germany risks dropping back in the global technological race behind the United States, Japan, and other parts of the world. Europe could become a backwater, financing the recovery of Russia and Eastern Europe at immense cost while the maritime powers race into a future that may be uncertain but brilliant. German companies, traditionally at the forefront of continental and global competitiveness, could not accept the notion that they have permanently fallen behind even if they have a safe local market.
- Finally, and perhaps most important, an American withdrawal from Europe again leaves Europe where it was before 1914 and before 1932. The American presence, for reasons that are perhaps impossible to explain, has been a stabilizing factor on the continent. It has also helped Germany to exercise its influence and preserve its interests without making enemies. Germany cannot contemplate an American departure without wondering about the effects it may well have for the future of Europe and Germany.

Aside from their questions about the United States, however, Chancellor Kohl and Minister Kinkel may also have their doubts about the usefulness of the global concert as a whole. Not only the U.S. government but other non-European G-7 members have shown with increasing frequency that they will not be prepared to do as much to help Eastern Europe and the remnants of the Soviet Union as Germany would like. Japan has not offered significant aid to Moscow, and the Kurile Islands dispute may be a welcome excuse for its reticence instead of a reason. Canada has already said that it will withdraw its troops from Germany and Europe. If the global concert will not act in Europe, Germany must act alone or with European partners.

The many speeches by German leaders about Germany's firm links with the West have not been intended to deceive their listeners. The speeches by former president Bush and by President Clinton about America's global interests are just as basic to their own thinking. But the forces that are now beginning to split the global concert along the Atlantic Ocean or along the English Channel are very powerful, and the best of intentions may not be able to offset them.

As indicated earlier, a German choice for Europe is really a choice for the shape of the world. While Germany decides, the world system remains in a state of suspended animation. That is why the G-7 summits that followed German unification were generally paralyzed. Little has been agreed on in either the commercial, the economic, or the strategic realm. Nor can anything be agreed on until Germany decides which way it wishes to turn.

The 1992 Munich summit was particularly fruitless, with far more public and private wrangling than agreement. The European continental states were most concerned about European issues—especially aid to Russia and the civil war in Yugoslavia. Some agreements were reached on those questions, although only very limited action was agreed upon. The maritime powers were more concerned with global questions, especially growth and the Uruguay Round. No agreements were reached on those questions. It appeared, however, that the maritime powers were more often in accord with each other than with the continental powers, and that England's prime minister, John Major, made several efforts to solve problems that Chancellor Kohl and President Mitterrand chose to leave alone.

A split in the world coalition poses a dilemma for the European maritime powers, especially Great Britain. London may have to choose between the European Community and the transatlantic world and may, as General Charles de Gaulle predicted, again choose the maritime powers—perhaps with some implications for the other maritime states in the European Community. At the very least, London will probably do more than any other European capital to prevent a split.

The G-7 format may again one day be productive if the European powers and Washington can jointly develop solutions to the disputes that have arisen across the Atlantic. If they cannot, the G-7 summits may become pieces of theater and the G-7 format an empty shell. For the global concert cannot function if continental Europe and the other members of the global system are not in accord on fundamentals.

At that point, Japan's role becomes crucial. For the past several years, as the trade disputes between the United States and France have simmered and boiled over, Japan has been waiting. It has not committed itself. It is trying to avoid isolation, although it remains under attack for its ever-growing export surplus. Unlike the Europeans, it has not confronted the United States on commercial questions and has suggested that it will contribute to a conclusion of the Uruguay Round when Washington and the EC resolve their differences. It clearly wants to continue to remain in the global system and the global concert.

The Japanese government has formally decided, despite reservations from other Asian governments, that Japanese forces can play a role in peace-keeping operations. The Japanese Diet has also committed itself to a policy of global assistance and support, offering the second largest contributions (after the United States) to international aid programs and the U.N. budget. Japan has been starting to play an important role in the G-7 despite its original reticence. It hosted the G-7 summit in 1993.

If Germany and Europe cannot settle their differences with America, Japan can and probably will take their place as America's principal collaborator in global affairs. The Japanese position is fundamentally different from the German, for Japan has no continent to draw it away from America. It may be more prepared than Germany to accommodate at least some American policy imperatives and to become a global partner.

A European-American split in the global concert may lead to a new and different kind of G-7, one that is divided between continental and maritime powers. There are three continental European members, Germany, France, and Italy, on the G-7, as well as three Atlantic maritime powers, the United States, Canada, and Great Britain—which is also a member of the European Community. Japan is the only Asian member to date, but it regards itself as a maritime power and might well join America. The existence of a separate European continental system and of a separate European consciousness can thus fundamentally change the board of directors of the global concert. The G-7 could become mainly a forum for negotiation and perhaps for confrontation between the continental Europeans and the other members.

This split in the global concert has immense implications for any new global balance. It divides the continental from the maritime powers. It divides the world of high wages and high aid and capital requirements from that of lower production costs and new technology. It also divides continental Europe, which now faces several potentially costly and severe crises, from the Americas and the Pacific, which are—at least for the moment—not confronted with parallel threats. A split could, therefore, damage the European continental powers more than the maritime powers. It could bring about the "Pacific century," superseding many centuries of Atlantic domination over world events.

A split creates problems for Germany itself. For only Germany has the resources to bring Eastern Europe and Russia into the twenty-first century—or, for that matter, into the twentieth—and Germany must be at the center of any continental system that has any hope of offering stability and prosperity. But, as it develops that kind of continental system, and as it commits its resources to that system, Germany cannot help but be pulled away from the opportunities of the global system that gave West Germany its opening to influence, prosperity and respectability.

As for the United States, the split will also present many problems, to the point where it could be seen as a major failure. It will show that American diplomacy, as in the past, could not deal with victory. The U.S. government and its political establishment will have proven too inflexible and uncompromising to allow a place for separate European structures or policies within a global system chaired by the United States. Forty years of U.S. commitment may have established a strong and united Europe, but it will have created an opponent rather than a partner in carrying the global burden. No American president could regard that as an achievement.

It goes without saying that a split in the global concert will change the nature of the German-American relationship. The United States, Japan, and others would then create a new and distinct forum in which they could meet separately from the continental Europeans, and Germany will again have lost a seat at the global table in return for its continental role.

If Germany retreats into Europe, the maritime powers will do what they have done before. They will pull away from their obligations and their installations on the shore, except perhaps for a token presence. They will concentrate on their own problems and on their relations with each other. They will leave the continental problems and the continental opportunities to the continental powers.

As in the past, the maritime powers will be spectators to events that can affect them deeply but that they will no longer be able to shape directly. They, like the continental powers, will have given up something of value and a significant measure of influence, but they may believe that they have gained a compensating measure of freedom from the burdens they carried for a long time.

A BILATERAL GERMAN-AMERICAN ALTERNATIVE?

Some Germans and Americans might hope that the two countries could maintain their mutual friendship and cooperation even if Europe as a whole were to split from the United States. For despite the arguments in the G-7 and elsewhere, Germany and the United States continue to have many common bilateral interests. Bonn and Washington consult constantly about an agenda that seems endless in its variety. Even as German-American disagreements are splattered across the headlines, German and American officials are meeting and working together on a daily basis, trying to solve problems and to coordinate their policies toward the innumerable complex and delicate matters that make up the fabric of the direct German-American relationship. The German and American bureaucracies manage the massive day-by-day agenda smoothly and diligently and in a positive spirit, even when they disagree.

Could bilateral German-American cooperation continue if the global concert splits or even begins to tear? Could the United States and Germany coordinate major policies bilaterally? Could they perhaps even serve as the main link between a continental and a maritime system, discussing and solving problems that arise between the two separate systems?

Such a pattern would change the nature of the relationship. West Germany and the United States cooperated mainly through and within multilateral institutions, not bilaterally. A direct bilateral relationship, especially one that links two separate and divergent systems, would be a major new departure for Bonn and Washington.

It may also be impossible. For the two states have still not reached the kind of relationship in which there is a true basis for an open dialogue and in which they can help each other carry responsibilities. The American government cannot justify a policy by arguing that it would please the German government, and the reverse may no longer be possible either.

The visits of President Richard von Weizsäcker to Washington in April 1992 and those of Chancellor Helmut Kohl to Camp David in April and to New York in May, 1992, as well as several other German-American discussions since 1990, show the difficulties facing a purely bilateral German-American relationship. They also show why it would not be wise for either government to count on it.

President von Weizsäcker's visit was given virtually no attention in Washington, certainly not at a level commensurate with that of the chief of state of the third most important country in the world. The visit received little coverage in the American media, far less than reports of skinheads in Germany. Even the national press that normally reports on foreign affairs paid it little heed. The press did, however, make a reference to the Nazi past. One press report recalled that there had been a protest when President von Weizsäcker had spoken at Harvard in 1987 because his father had been a convicted war criminal.

The American press remains more fascinated by the "bad German" than by the "good German." It is prepared if necessary to paint the good German bad. Thus a man widely respected in Germany and elsewhere was presented to Washington readers as the son of a criminal, and the creditable story of his family was not told.

Many American press and television reports on Germany dwell on the links rather than on the contrast between the German past and the German present. References to Germany's Nazi past are a staple of virtually every discussion of current German affairs, and many analysts strive to find connections between that past and the present. It was only the massive antirightist demonstrations by hundreds of thousands of German citizens during the winter of 1992–1993 that made many Americans realize that the new Germany was different from the old Germany.

When President John F. Kennedy came to Berlin in 1963, governing mayor Willy Brandt told him that the day would come when Germans would no longer make an extra bow when they entered a room because of the memory of the Holocaust. That time has come—if not for older Germans, at least for the younger generation—because young Germans also see America's faults. But the psychological burden on both sides of dealing with the lingering memories remains a political weight on the total relationship. It complicates any German-American bilateralism even when individual Germans and Americans find it pleasant and productive to deal directly with each other.

But the press itself was not alone to blame for von Weizsäcker's reception. Not only were other events—like riots in Los Angeles—distracting its attention, but the official greeting for the German president was at best tepid. Few senators or representatives attended his speech to a joint session of the U.S. Congress. Even the White House and the State Department did not make a major effort to background and highlight the visit as an important call by a singularly important friend.

If the German president wanted to thank the American people for German unity, few influential Americans were there to pay attention, and few were there to hear him ask America to stay in Europe or to reflect and report on his plea. The U.S. government made no special effort to stress the importance of the new and powerful "partner in leadership" and certainly did not establish the setting for a new and important global interlocutor.

In the American political dialogue, German-bashing is on a par with Japan-bashing. Germany is all too often described—as is Japan—as a country that owes America a great debt for its protection and that has not repaid that debt. But the German government has never created the kinds of institutional links and structures in Washington and elsewhere in the United States that Japan has established. Germany is, therefore, even more vulnerable than Japan to criticism. It was only in the late 1980s that Chancellor Kohl's government began establishing university centers for German studies. Many accusations against Germany remain unchallenged and unanswered in the American media, and particularly in the American capital.

If the American government did not take the German president seriously enough, the German government did not take the American president seriously enough. At Camp David, Chancellor Kohl's refusal to support President Bush on GATT showed that he regarded Germany's relations with France to be more important than the wishes (and perhaps even the electoral needs) of his American partner. When the chancellor spoke in New York to the Association of American Newspaper Publishers on May 5, 1992, he repeated the assurances of German-American friendship as he had done at Camp David, insisting that "Europe still needs America," but he did not say what Bush needed to hear. And only a few weeks after his visit to Camp David, Chancellor Kohl met with President Mitterrand in France to announce the agreement for the Franco-German Corps although he knew that President Bush strongly opposed the creation of such a force. Although the chancellor pushed through a major reform of the EC Common Agricultural Policy in May of 1992, it did not provide sufficient basis for an agreement that Bush could defend in an election year.

All too often, even at this crucial and decisive time, it appears as though the United States and Germany take each other for granted. They do not appear to make special efforts to recognize each other's particular needs and interests. Nor do they act as if they are ready to cooperate in solving major global issues constructively.

This lack of mutual attention has actually increased since unification. Before 1990, no major question in Bonn would be decided without an analysis of its effect on German-American relations, and no major question in Washington would be decided without an analysis of its effect on the American position in Germany and Europe. But such analyses may no longer be made, and if they are, the results are certainly ignored.

Bonn may find a direct bilateral relationship with the United States even more difficult than Washington might find it. One of the reasons senior levels of the German government did not feel comfortable with George Bush's essentially bilateral concept of German-American "partners in leadership" was the implication that it meant a singular German association with the United States. The notion of a direct German-American alliance remains difficult for Germany to accept. In both Bonn and Washington, therefore, there is no adequate basis for an exclusively or predominantly bilateral link.

In fact, the new united Germany also appears to have trouble reconciling its new position with its past dependence on the United States. The American press reported that at the Rio de Janeiro environmental summit in June, 1992, the German delegation consistently made a point of letting the press know that the German record on the environment and the German role at the summit were much more positive than the American contributions. These statements created the impression that Germany needed to demonstrate its new influence and importance by showing that it was not only independent but also opposed to U.S. policies.

A united Germany may thus need to establish its new identity by showing its independence from the United States as a sign of authority and autonomy rather than by tying itself more closely to the United States.

A long time may have to pass before Germany and the United States develop the kind of easy and relaxed relationship that exists between America and a few others, a relationship that absorbs and survives specific differences and maintains a balance of friendship. It may never come. Nor may a German-American link that could bridge any differences between Europe and the United States.

Three major states in Europe can have a strong, direct, and mutually respectful link with America:

- Great Britain, which has long had it in the "special relationship" that has continued during almost the entire twentieth century. Prime Minister Major has made a special effort to cultivate it, both in his direct dealings with Presidents Bush and Clinton as well as in the role he has tried to play internationally—as in Munich.
- France (paradoxically, despite its disagreements with Washington), as the home of the Marquis de Lafayette, the site of the 1789 revolution, and the allied land where countless Americans fought and many still lie buried.

- Russia, which has been led in the recent past by personalities that have won considerable admiration in the United States. Boris Yeltsin, despite initial skepticism in Washington, had a powerful effect during his visit in June, 1992, in part by showing that the Russian government had broken with the Communist past. There is also a long-standing mutual fascination between the Russian and American people, a fascination that transcended the cold war. Most important, perhaps, the Russian and American governments now share a common strategic bond in the management of their nuclear arsenals, although they also have many political differences and conflicts of interest across the world.

One of the ironies of German support for French continental concepts in Europe is that France's bilateral link with America will remain in place and will perhaps even be strengthened while the German structural links may be jeopardized.

France has many sentimental ties with America. For example, the fiftieth anniversary of the D-Day landings in June, 1994, will rekindle a powerful bond between the French and the Americans. France is also a permanent member of the U.N. Security Council and a nuclear power. President Mitterrand has not hesitated to drive that point home by calling for meetings of the nuclear club, meetings that have deliberately and demonstrably excluded Germany. It was the American government that on several occasions either blocked such gatherings or reduced their significance in order not to offend Germany, even as the German government was supporting France in other debates.

Washington may well decide that France is the European state that can make decisions and can affect the future, whereas Germany only follows and will not push on Washington's behalf. Washington, like other capitals, prefers allies that can and do deliver. If France is dominant, American officials will talk to French officials instead of Germans when they need to solve problems with Europe or in the G-7. The Germans, by following France, may have persuaded Washington that Paris is now more important than Bonn. Paris may, with Bonn's help, become Washington's main partner on the continent. That was not true during most of the cold war, when Bonn was Washington's major European partner.

Despite the difficulties facing a bilateral German-American relationship, however, it may be precisely the kind of link that must now be created as the older structural ties decline and if the global concert splits. But there should be no illusions about the determination required to achieve it. Several European states will oppose it. Many Americans may not be able to manage it because they are too accustomed to having Germany follow rather than lead. And many Germans may not be able to manage it because they may fear that they are being permanently relegated to junior partnership. No other task of German and American statesmanship over the next ten years may be more necessary or more difficult.

GERMANY CAN AND DOES SAY NO

The most dangerous moment in any relationship is when a mutually recognized and long-established balance of power between the partners shifts, especially if it shifts precipitately. Unification brought about such a shift in the German-American balance in the space of a year. Although Germany's weight in the relationship had been growing for decades, neither the German nor the American government and nation were prepared for the suddenness and the size of the shift. They have not yet adjusted to it.

From being a junior partner, an outpost of the global concert within Central Europe, Germany has suddenly become a full partner. Its circle of influence and power in Europe East and West gives Germany a powerfully reinforcing echo that makes some of its policies more important than America's.

Even before unification, West German and American interests and policies differed on occasion. There were arguments about many issues, especially about economic policy and about the implementation of the common strategic interests. But the West German government often had to adjust, except in such areas as finance, where it was primarily making domestic policy even when it had an international effect. The new Germany no longer needs to do so. It can and does say no.

A no from united Germany is stronger, more credible, more important, and more sustainable than a West German no. It can be affirmed even under pressure. It will be more widely felt. It can and will shape the world.

If George Bush hoped in 1990 that the German unification he had supported so strongly in NATO would create a new and powerful global partner and a consistently congenial and supportive interlocutor, he could legitimately have asked himself later whether his expectations had been met. The first two years after unification have not offered an auspicious start. And if Bill Clinton thought that the new Germany would be like the old, he was also due for a surprise.

By the same token, if Helmut Kohl expected that the U.S. government would continue to support the newly united Germany as closely as it had previously supported the Western portions of divided Germany and Berlin, he must also have suffered a shock. For the Americans showed themselves in some ways more demanding than before, even as they were withdrawing from Europe. They were asking Germany to play roles (as in the Gulf and the GATT) that it was not ready to play, and they sometimes scolded Germany in public even when the United States was also at fault.

Neither country and neither government is really prepared for this situation. Bonn is no longer ready to follow. Washington is not yet ready to share with Germany the decisions on vital matters. It may consult with the German government, but the U.S. decision process is so complicated that Americans do not like to be told that others disagree with their policies and that they must go through internal coordination again.

In particular, American officials are not yet prepared to listen to Germans as patiently and as respectfully as they may listen to the British, Japanese, Russians, or French. They are not prepared to hear Germany listen more closely to others than to Washington. Nor are they always prepared to take German domestic political needs as seriously as those of others. The frequent American references to German "assertiveness" reflect that kind of attitude, as does the American habit—which the Germans find frustrating—of putting a different interpretation on German actions than on those of other states.

Germans are so accustomed to having American support for their ideas and policies that they are sometimes astonished when the United States does not support them. Bonn has to accept that when it acts on its own policies, Washington will not feel obliged to support its dependent ally as much as in the past. By the same token, the German government must learn to live with the full effects, implications, and consequences of its policies.

Washington may be wrong or right on one or another dispute, but it must look at the totality of the differences with Bonn and wonder if these reflect a new attitude rather than isolated disagreements. Bonn, in turn, has to wonder if its ally is overreacting, for it is not accustomed to having its acts shape the world and Europe as much as they are now beginning to do. That is why German officials who visit Washington insist that German-American relations remain good even if no agreements are reached on any major topic.

Europe is now Germany's clear priority, and other things will have to wait. America, perhaps looking for excuses to reduce its own obligations, may now see this as a sign that it can accelerate its own withdrawals and disengage from at least some of its commitments. It must certainly see Germany's new priorities as a sign that Germany is no longer prepared to accept U.S. concepts regarding the functioning of the European or global system.

Those who believe that German-American relations must be the backbone of any world order, old or new, see this stage in relations as a most dangerous moment, reflecting a most misguided set of mutual attitudes. But the importance of the German-American relationship has clearly not been great enough to persuade either state to conduct itself in a way that will protect that relationship.

Even as Germany is increasingly going its own way, America is not offering a handle by which Germany can easily continue to link itself to the global concert. Instead, it is often impatiently placing demands that the Germans cannot meet. Germany reacts by further distancing itself, creating structures that will slowly draw away from the global system.

One cannot help but have the impression that the Americans, long accustomed to having Bonn as an increasingly powerful but still dependent partner, do not know how to adjust to having that same partner become more important and independent. They seem unable to acknowledge that Germany is now one of the world's most important states. They often act as if it were still a semidependent client. They seem much more prepared to see Germany as a small state than as a powerful one.

By the same token, the Germans seem to have difficulty acknowledging that America may at times need support as much as others do. As indicated earlier, Kohl was much more prepared to do what President Mitterrand needed than what President Bush needed. If America does not know what to do with a relatively more powerful friend, Germany does not know what to do with a less powerful friend, to find a way of helping without being dependent.

The United States and Germany have not learned how to manage equality. The American government still believes that Germany will and even must agree with the United States on all major questions and that Germany will support Washington's views. It still regards Bonn as a junior partner. The German government, for its part, is more ready to take a separate path, but it still does not fully understand that its decisions can actually shape the world as a whole and not only its own immediate interests. In a way, it also still regards itself as a junior partner, although a more independent one. The Americans are not prepared to relinquish responsibility; the Germans are not prepared to accept it. Neither appears to understand that they now must take joint and perhaps fully equal responsibility.

Neither Washington nor Bonn wants a crisis in German-American relations. Any such crisis would be unintentional. The governments and their leaders want to remain close friends. Neither Chancellor Kohl nor President Clinton want to jeopardize the alliance or to split the global concert. Yet they appear powerless to stop themselves or others from taking actions that disrupt their mutual relationship and that are sufficiently important to lead precisely to the crisis that they wish to avoid.

Throughout all this, much of the German-American dialogue remains stilted, lost in the sentimental language and rituals of the past forty years and not moving into the language and the agenda of the new relationship that must follow. Too much romanticism about "old German-American ties" may, in fact, jeopardize the new ties that must be created. Some kind of German-American relationship will still be necessary for a stable world, but it must be built on new foundations and it will probably have to be based on a mutual recognition of agreements and disagreements rather than on traditional reassurances that all is well when it is not.

It is the particular curse of the German-American relationship that these countries cannot be neutral about each other. There is no halfway house in which they can afford to ignore each other. What each does affects the other, directly or indirectly, especially in economic matters but in other areas as well. They are both too important to the world, and to each other's interests.

What is perhaps most striking about this trend is the paralysis afflicting policymakers on both sides. Whereas German and American leaders from the 1940s through the 1980s and even into the early 1990s solved problems and created institutions so that they might cooperate, they now drift and do not act. All too often, when problems develop, they do not discuss them frankly and do not solve them, preferring to pretend that all is well.

They must find such solutions, however, for they must continue to cooperate if they genuinely want to shape a world that suits their common as well as separate interests. For the United States and Germany still need each other for many essential purposes. They will have as many common interests in the coming century as they have in the second half of the twentieth century, even if those interests are not the same.

The United States and Germany now have the joint opportunity to use the global concert in order to build the policies and structures that will succeed the cold war and bring the world successfully and cooperatively into the twenty-first century. In that future world, they should be able to agree and to coordinate in establishing a peaceful global political order, a truly prosperous economic order, and a common global defense structure that could help deter as well as win conflicts.

To do that, however, they must recognize two very clear requirements:

- The United States must take Germany more seriously, because German actions now have wider consequences. The United States must pay more attention to German views but must also make certain that its own actions will not be misinterpreted in Germany.
- Germany must also take itself more seriously. For it can destroy what it worked hard to build. It can also provoke new and different reactions in America from those that it might have provoked in the past.

Before German unification, the German and American governments could both be confident that their disagreements would not genuinely affect the global concert. Germany could even go its own way if it chose, for its departure from the global concert would not destroy the world order maintained by the United States. Now, it is different. A German decision to go its own way—or to go with a new European order against a global order led by the United States—would alter the world order and could destroy the global concert.

As neither Germany nor America now need each other as obviously as before, but still need each other fundamentally, they must find new ways not only to maintain their cooperation but also to explain that cooperation to their publics and to their other allies.

The evidence since German unification, however, is the opposite. It indicates a clear danger that they will not work together but will separate from each other and will split the worldwide system that united them and gave them both their strength. Having created brilliantly successful structures, they may be unable either to transform them or to use them in the new world. In that case, the world will not advance into the twenty first century but will slide back into the nineteenth.

If Germany and the United States cannot find the basis for a new relationship that reflects the new realities of their association, they must and will separate. They are, therefore, at a crucial point.

If and when they separate, the effect on global affairs can be massive. Germany will not be an enemy of the United States, as it was in the world wars, but it will be an alternative center of power around which others—especially continental Europeans—can assemble and coalesce. It will destroy America's ability to carry out certain global policies, and it will sometimes counteract and cancel out the effects of U.S. policies.

The global concert will then split. The European members will pull away from the North American and Asian members. It is uncertain whether Great Britain will join Europe or the United States at that point, and whether the global concert will split in the Atlantic or in the English Channel.

In that process, however, Germany will also jeopardize its own influence and freedom to act. For the more powerful and independent Germany appears, the less powerful and independent it really is. Other Europeans will regard it with greater suspicion than they do now. And the United States will look to France, Russia, and Great Britain as its interlocutors on and near the European continent.

There may even be a sharp but troubling historical parallel between the German determination to make France its principal ally and the policy pursued by the Berlin government a century earlier. Then, England wanted to develop a closer link with Germany but the German government preferred a continental partner, Austria-Hungary. Germany thus declined a firm connection to the global concert, a connection that was only established after World War II with new and different partners.

This alliance had been Germany's great strategic mistake before World War I and had perhaps been the mistake that made World War I inevitable. It had compelled Germany to guarantee its own security by arrangements that had threatened or appeared to threaten others. It had also compelled Germany to support the European interests of its continental allies as if they had been its own, forcing it to back Austria in the Balkans.

The link between America and Germany, between the great sea-power and the great land-power, had broken the vicious cycle and had put German (as well as American) security on a stable footing. The link should not be abandoned without the most careful consideration, for Germany's security is at stake. So, oddly enough, is France's security, for France has actually been able to enjoy a more stable Europe through the German-American connection than it might have been able to create on its own. The French search for a Franco-German alternative to the German-American link may turn out to be very shortsighted.

But the loss of Germany as its main continental ally also represents a defeat for the United States, and it also has an ominous historical parallel. For the global concert needs friends on the continents, and especially in Europe. And if America chooses to withdraw completely from Europe instead of keeping or seeking strong allies on the continent, America will be repeating the mistake of its isolation after World War I.

Such a split between the global concert and the European continent would thus represent a mistake of historic proportions for both Germany and the United States.

No alliance can travel only on momentum and promises. Sooner or later, it will become irrelevant to the partners and they will become irrelevant to each other. A rupture will come not because they have sought it. It will come because their relationship did not have the same priority that it had before and because the automatic corrective processes on which they long relied no longer operate as before.

The cold war global coalition will have collapsed, as coalitions do when wars are won, and the current global concert must and will disintegrate as the central directing structure for the world. A new one may be shaped over time, but its membership cannot now be foreseen.

The disintegration of the global concert will damage both Germany and the United States. It will again leave Germany where it was throughout most of its history—outside the world's major alliances and without a reliable link to the maritime powers. It will end any American claim to be the world's remaining superpower, for no state can be a superpower if it does not have a connection to continental Europe. Both states will have lost the association that guaranteed their political, military, and economic security.

When Germany begins to find its main friends on the European continent, and when the United States begins again to see its principal true European interlocutors outside Bonn and Berlin, German and American actions will still affect each other. But they will jeopardize each other's interests, not support them. For even if some of their broad objectives remain identical, their policies will differ too much to hold them together.

Then the day must come, and will come, when words begin to mirror divergent views more sharply than they now do, and when policy differences will no longer be covered by polite talk.

When that day comes, the alliance that anchored the Western system and that defeated Communism will pass into history. Those who shaped it will mourn, as will some of those who let it be destroyed. But it will still fade, along with other memories of the cold war, of the wide arch that spanned the Atlantic, and of the great intercontinental edifice that reached from the Sea of Japan to the Elbe and the Spree.

ABOUT THE BOOK
AND AUTHOR

When George Bush and the Department of State supported the reunification of Germany in 1989, they fully expected that a new united Germany would support American foreign policy and help maintain the global alliance system as "partners in leadership." Since unification, however, the United States is discovering that its relationship with Germany can be complex and unpredictable.

The course Germany is charting in politics, economics, and defense is steering away from close cooperation with the United States. In fact, united Germany has yet to join the United States wholeheartedly in solving any single major international problem. German chancellor Kohl offered only financial aid during the Gulf War, he has sided with the French government to promote a separate European army, and he has not expedited agreement on the Uruguay Round of trade talks. The new Germany is not simply a larger version of the old West Germany. No longer a junior partner, its power, prestige, and priorities have shifted profoundly.

At the same time, the United States has turned its focus inward, beset by domestic issues that have given the American people new worries and new priorities. Many want to pull back most U.S. forces from Europe. They believe it is time for the Europeans, and especially the Germans, to take responsibility for their own problems. Furthermore, neo-Nazi riots and ethnic brutality in Germany have fueled American preoccupation with the Germany of the past.

In this brisk extended essay, Smyser, a widely respected Germany-watcher, shows how Germany and America, the backbone of the Atlantic alliance and of the global system, may now split apart. He argues that such a drastic shift would have immense implications for any new world order, dividing, once again, the maritime from the continental powers.

W. R. Smyser is one of America's leading experts on German affairs. He is the author of a book on the German economy and of several earlier books on German-American relations. He writes frequently for American and German magazines and newspapers. He teaches at Georgetown University and at the U.S. Foreign Service Institute.

INDEX